Play Bridge Now

Play
Bridge
Now

Montgomery Coe

Cardoza Publishing

ABOUT THE AUTHOR

Montgomery Coe, the author of *The Basics of Winning Bridge*, is an experienced and well-respected bridge teacher who has introduced tens of thousands of players to the game of bridge.

Library of Congress Catalog Card No: 2017948788
ISBN: 978-1-58042-357-1

Visit our website or write for a full list of Cardoza Publishing books and advanced strategies.

CARDOZA PUBLISHING

P.O. Box 98115, Las Vegas, NV 89193
Toll-Free Phone (800)577-WINS
email: cardozabooks@aol.com
www.cardozabooks.com

TABLE OF CONTENTS

1. INTRODUCTION

Bridge is one of the most popular games ever invented. Since its introduction in 1926, it has attracted millions of players. It's truly an international game, played in every country of the world.

There are a number of good reasons for the popularity of bridge. First, it's a partnership game, and this social aspect differentiates it from games in which an individual plays against other individuals, such as poker. Second, unlike many other card games, bridge can be played for pure enjoyment, without a profit motive. The game requires a great deal of skill, combined, of course, with a little luck. In some forms of bridge—such as duplicate, where teams of four play against each other—it's a game of pure skill. With the challenge of bridge being to build your skill, there's no need for the game to be played for money.

There's no end to the possibilities and pleasures of this great game. When four bridge players get together, the can arrange various partnerships or playing set-ups, or the partnerships can be fixed. When partners play together regularly, they can enter tournaments and win master points and titles.

The most common version of bridge is called **rubber bridge**. This is the home version of contract bridge, and my emphasis in this book will be on this version of the game. As your skill at bridge increases, you can use the same principles that I will teach you about rubber bridge and apply them to duplicate bridge, which is the format for tournaments. I will fully explain the difference between these versions during the course of the book.

The game of bridge has two distinct parts, both of which you must master in order to play it skillfully. The first part of the game is the bidding, in which the partners attempt to reach a contract that they can make. The second part is the play of the hand. Both parts are of equal importance. In this book, I'm going to take you step-by-step through each process, so that you'll be able to play the game at a competent and skillful level.

What I'm going to do is teach you the game from the very beginning. If you know nothing at all about bridge, don't worry. Everything you need to know to play the game is contained in this book. And even readers who are somewhat familiar with the game can benefit from a review of correct bidding and playing skills. My aim is to improve your bridge ability, so that you can enjoy this fascinating game to the utmost. No matter what level of skill you have at bridge, this book will make you a better player.

I will show you how to score your bridge game, and how to use various bidding conventions, finesses, and all the other standard bridge maneuvers that will enable you to understand and enjoy bridge to its fullest. Bridge is a fascinating game, and players who have played all their lives still find something new each time the game is dealt. There are truly millions of possible hands that can come up in any deal, and the challenges of bridge are always fresh and new. Certainly this has contributed to its immense popularity.

So, whether you're planning to play bridge at home or in tournaments, by the time you finish this book, you'll be fully prepared to be a winner at bridge!

2. RULES OF PLAY

The Partnership

One of the unique qualities of bridge is that it is a partnership game in which the partners—within certain limits—are able to signal the strength of their hands during the bidding as well as during the playing of a hand. Bridge is a game played by four players. They form two sets of partners; one partnership is known as **East** and **West**, and the other is known as **North** and **South**. Any diagrammed bridge hand will adhere to that format and set up the hands as follows:

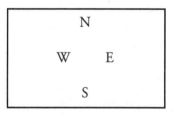

As you can see from the diagram, the partners sit opposite each other. The result of the play is shared equally by each pair of partners, and one score is kept for each partnership. Thus, if East and West bid and make one club, the score would be twenty points for East-West, not twenty points for East and twenty points for West. Because of the partnership aspect of bridge, the partners must cooperate with each other during the bidding and, when defending the contract, during the playing out of the hands.

Bridge is basically an unselfish game, in which a player must sublimate his interests for the good of the partnership. If you play with this selfless attitude, you'll be a good partner, and you'll add to the enjoyment of the game.

Cards

A bridge game uses a standard fifty-two card deck, without the jokers. In the course of a game of rubber bridge, players generally use two decks. While one is being dealt, the other (usually with a different colored back) is being shuffled and made ready for the next deal. The standard method is for the dealer's partner to shuffle the other deck, then place it to the right of the player between the dealer and shuffler—in other words, next to the player who will deal next.

Ranks of the Cards

The standard deck of cards consists of four suits: spades, hearts, diamonds and clubs, and there are thirteen cards within each suit. In bridge, the ace is the highest ranking card, followed by the king, queen, jack, 10, 9, 8, 7, 6, 5, 4, 3, and 2 (the lowest ranking of all the cards). In this book, you'll see me abbreviate the cards as follows: A (ace), K (king), Q (queen), and J (jack). I will show the numbered cards by their numbers.

The Deal

The deal moves in a clockwise fashion, with each player dealing once every four games. If you played a game in which South was the first dealer, then West would deal next, followed by North, and finally East.

Before dealing, the dealer gives the cards to the player to his right. That player cuts the cards, and the dealer then restacks them and proceeds to deal. If South is the dealer, the first card will be dealt to West, then a card to North, a card to East and finally a card to South, himself. The cards are dealt face down, and all cards are dealt. Thus, at the end of the deal, each player will have thirteen cards.

Until all cards have been dealt, other players should not pick up any of their cards. If there's been a mistake in the deal, and one player has received too many or too few cards, this can be remedied—*as long as the cards haven't been seen by the players.* Once players have looked at their cards, a mistake would result in a misdeal, which would mean that a new deal would have to be made.

Sorting the Cards

After all the cards have been dealt, the players pick up their cards and sort them by suits. Within the suits, you'll want to sort your cards by their relative rank, from highest to lowest. Bridge is a game in which the bidding and playing out of cards is by suits, and it's therefore helpful to hold your cards by suits. A typical holding might look like this:

♠ A 10 8 5   ♥ 9 7   ♦ J 9 8   ♣ K Q 3 2

Rank of Suits

In contract bridge, the suits have a definite value both in bidding and scoring. The highest-ranking suit is spades, followed by hearts, diamonds, and, finally, clubs. Spades and hearts are known as the **major suits**; diamonds and clubs are the **minor suits**. In scoring, as you'll see later, the major suits are accorded thirty points each, while the minor suits receive only twenty points.

Because of the different ranks of the suits, the bidding follows a specific order. The lowest bid of any suit is in clubs. Diamonds are next, followed by hearts, and spades are the highest bid of a suit. A bid of one club can be followed by a bid of one diamond, one heart, or one spade. A bid of one diamond can be followed by a bid or one heart or one spade. A bid of one heart can be followed by a bid of one spade. But if a bid of one spade is made, since spades is the highest-ranking suit, the next bid will have to be at the two level. You cannot have a bid of one spade followed by a bid of one heart. The bidder of hearts would have to bid at least two hearts.

No-Trump

Bridge contracts can be made in the four suits, but they can also be made in no-trump. **No-trump** is just what its name implies:

none of the suits is trump. As you'll see, when a final bid is made in the course of the bidding, that bid determines the trump suit. For example, if the final bid were four spades, then spades would be trump. If the final bid were five clubs, then clubs would be trump. However, if the final bid were three no-trump, then there would be no trump suit.

No-trump is the highest possible bid at any level. To refresh your memory, the highest suit you can bid is spades. If someone has bid one spade, another player can then bid one no trump, since no trump is a higher bid than any of the suits.

Trumps

One of the purposes of bidding is for a partnership to have the final say in which suit will be trump (or if the partnership so prefers, to play out the hand in no-trump). When a particular suit is trump, that suit is more powerful than any other suit during the playing of the hand.

When a player is **void** in a suit—that is, has no more of a particular suit which is not trump, he can play a trump to win the trick. I'll go into this in greater detail later. For now, it's important that you remember that trump is the strongest of all suits while a hand is being played.

For example, let's say diamonds are trump on a hand. One player leads the ace of hearts. The next player plays the queen of hearts, and the third player plays the jack of hearts. If the fourth player is void in hearts, he can play the 2 of diamonds (a trump) and win the trick.

Object of the Game

The object of bridge is to bid for a particular contract and then win enough rounds of cards—known as **tricks**—to justify your bid. If a partnership bids and makes as many or more tricks than the bid called for, the partnership will be rewarded with points. If it fails to make the tricks needed to justify the bid, it is said to **go down,** or **be set,** and the other side is awarded points.

Basics of Bidding

Contract bridge, as I have mentioned, is divided into two distinct parts. First there is the bidding, and then there's the playing of the hand. The purpose of bidding is to reach a contract that you can make for maximum scoring. The ideal contract gives the partnership bidding it the highest number of points based on the strengths of the two hands of the partnership. Sometimes you'll find that both partnerships have rather strong hands. Then the bidding becomes competitive, and each partnership tries to put in the final bid so that they can determine what suit will be trump (or establish no-trump if they prefer it).

The lowest possible bid is at the **one-level,** such as "one heart." When a bidder makes this bid, he is essentially saying that he has a strong enough hand to open the bidding, and if the bid ends at one heart, with all other players passing, he can make seven tricks by playing out the hand.

The reason he has to make seven tricks, rather than just the one trick he bid, is that the first six tricks are collectively called **book.** It is assumed in bridge that all bids are added onto book to determine how many tricks a partnership must win to make the contract. A bid of three no-trump means that the bidding partnership must win nine tricks. A bid of seven clubs means that the bidding partnership must win all thirteen tricks—and not lose any tricks at all. When such a bid and contract is made, it is known as a **grand slam.**

Let's return to the ranks of suits. You can see that the lowest possible bid that can be made is one club, and the highest possible bid is seven no-trump. Suit and no-trump bids are not the only bids that can be made. A player may pass and not make any suit or no-trump bid. If a player passes, he may still come back and make another bid of a suit, no-trump or double when the bidding returns to him. A double is usually a bid made to penalize the opposing partnership when a player feels that they have bid the wrong suit, shouldn't have bid no-trump, or have bid too high. He's doubling because he believes that they cannot win enough tricks to fulfill their contract. To review, a **trick** is a round of play in which each participant plays one card from his hand. Altogether there are thirteen tricks to be played and won.

There are other possible reasons for bidding a double, but I'll cover them in the appropriate sections. For now, you should know that a double is another valid bid open to the bidders. After a double is bid by the opposing partnership, a player can redouble. A redouble means that the player redoubling believes that the double bid was in error and that he can fulfill his contract.

Let's review all the possible bids that can be made in contract bridge. First, there's a suit bid, then a no-trump bid, a pass, a double, and a redouble. Let's follow an imaginary session of bidding to see how these bids can be made. To start off, we'll look at a diagram of the four players involved in the bidding. The first player to bid is the dealer. The (D) next to South will indicate that he is the dealer (and thus the first to bid).

Bidding always moves clockwise. In the diagram below, South would bid first, then West, then North, then East. The bidding ends when there are three consecutive passes after the last bid.

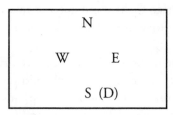

SOUTH	WEST	NORTH	EAST
One heart	Pass	One spade	Two clubs
Two spades	Pass	Four spades	Double
Pass	Pass	Redouble	Pass
Pass	Pass		

In the above bidding sequence, South opened the bidding with a bid of "One heart," which shows a fairly strong hand. If he had a weak hand, he could have passed. West, who was next to bid, passed and continued to pass during the entire bidding sequence. It was his partner, East, who doubled the contract bid of four spades. His double was answered with a redouble by North, the original bidder of spades. After the redouble, there were three passes, which ended the bidding. Whenever there are three passes after a bid of a suit, no-trump, double or redouble, the bidding ends.

If all the players have weak hands, and they all pass on the opening round of bidding, the bidding ceases, and all the players throw in their cards. The sequence would look like this:

WEST (D)	NORTH	EAST	SOUTH
Pass	Pass	Pass	Pass

A double or redouble keeps the bidding alive, and there may be more bids after that one. The next sequence of bids shows this situation. North is the dealer.

NORTH (D)	EAST	SOUTH	WEST
Pass	One diamond	One spade	Two hearts
Three clubs	Double	Redouble	Three hearts
Pass	Pass	Pass	

After the redouble by South, West still had a chance to bid three hearts. The three subsequent passes ended the bidding.

Tricks

I have mentioned the taking of tricks, or the winning of tricks. To remind you, a trick is a round in which all four players play a card. If all four players have the suit led, the highest ranking card of the suit wins the trick. For example, suppose South led the 9♣. By **led**, I mean that he was the first to play a card on a particular round. If West played the 4♣, North played the Q♣, and East played the 5♣, then North would win that trick, since the queen is the highest ranking of the cards played on that round.

Altogether, there are thirteen tricks to be won, one for every card the players hold. Each of the players must be aware of the potential for taking tricks with the cards in his hand, especially the partners who bid a particular contract. By **contract**, I mean the final bid, which determines just how many tricks the partnership must win to gain points.

If the final bid is at the four level, then the partnership must win ten tricks to make or fulfill the contract (remember that the first six tricks are called "book"). The partners can also win more than ten tricks; that enables them to get extra points in the scoring. At least ten tricks must be won, or they score nothing. The defenders—the other partnership—will endeavor to win at least four tricks to **set** or defeat the contract. If the defenders win at least four tricks, points will be awarded to them.

During the bidding, it's therefore important that you know (to the best of your ability) just how many tricks can be won with both your and your partner's cards. Special emphasis is placed on high ranking cards and trumps, which are important cards for taking in tricks. As you may recall, one of the goals of bidding is to name the suit that will be trump. Whatever the final bid is in a suit, that suit automatically becomes trump. Thus, if the final bid is two diamonds, diamonds is the trump suit. If the final bid is four hearts, hearts is the trump suit, and so forth. When the final bid is in no-trump, then no suit can be used as trump; all suits are equally strong.

One of the powerful uses of trump is when a player is void in a led suit. For example, if spades is the trump suit, and a player is void in clubs, if a club is led, he can play a trump on it at his discretion. He'll win the trick, no matter what the rank of his trump. If a 10, queen and ace of clubs had been played, and the last player to put down a card were void in clubs, by playing any spade (the trump suit), he will win the trick. I mentioned that he may play a trump at his discretion—when a player is void in a suit, he can also play any other suit, but those will be losers. Only a trump will win the trick.

Let's follow an example of "trumping" a trick. Spades is the trump suit. The 3♦ is led, and the next two players play the 7♦ and the K♦. The last player to play has no more diamonds—he is "void in diamonds." He plays the 2♠—trumping the trick—and he wins it.

Suppose he instead elects not to trump the suit with the spades he holds. Instead he plays a club. Since he didn't follow suit and didn't play a trump, he cannot win the trick. The trick is won instead by the highest ranking of the diamonds—the king.

Basics of Play

Let us assume the following sequence of bids:

SOUTH	WEST	NORTH	EAST
One spade	Pass	Two spades	Pass
Four spades	Pass	Pass	Pass

The bidding is now complete, since there were three passes after the bid of four spades by South. The contract is in four spades, and thus spades is the trump suit. Since South first bid spades, he is the **declarer**—the person who plays the hand for the successful bidders. West and East are now the defenders, and they're hoping to win enough tricks to set the contract. The bidding has been completed, and it is now time to play the hand.

The first lead is always made by the player to the declarer's left. In contract bridge, the defenders always lead first, which is a big advantage for them. For all tricks thereafter, the winner of the previous trick has the next lead.

In the contract we just established, West leads the first card. Once West plays a card, North, South's partner, will put all of his cards face up on the table. They will remain face up for all to see throughout the playing of the thirteen tricks. North is now called the **dummy**, and he no longer participates in the game. The declarer (South) now makes all the plays for the offense, including the cards in dummy's hand.

After West has played his first card, the declarer now selects a card from dummy's hand to play. Then East plays a card, and finally the declarer puts down the fourth card on that round of play. The first trick has been played and won by one or the other of the partnerships. Whoever won the trick now plays first, and then everyone else follows in clockwise order. The winner of that next trick again plays first, and play progresses in this fashion until all thirteen tricks have been played out.

After thirteen tricks have been played, each side counts its winning tricks. To fulfill his contract, South must have won at least ten tricks. If he has, he makes his contract. If he won less than ten tricks, he is said to be *set*, and West and East score points for setting the contract.

When that hand has ended, it is West's turn to deal. He deals out the thirteen cards to each player, and bidding starts anew. Since I've mentioned the idea of scoring points to you, let's now take a look at scoring in contract bridge.

3. SCORING: GAME AND RUBBER

Scoresheet

At the end of each game, the score of that game is entered on a scoresheet, which looks like this:

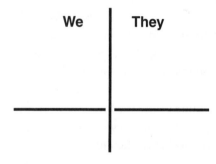

Usually, one of the partnerships keep score, and its score is "We." The score for the opposing partnership is set as "They." The partnership, not the individual players, is credited with the point score.

The horizontal line is an important separation in scoring. Only scores for tricks bid and made go below the horizontal line. All other scores, such as overtricks, penalties, or honors, go above the line. I will fully explain these scores later in this chapter.

The only way a partnership can get points below the line is if it is the declaring side. The defenders cannot score below the line.

Trick Scores

Tricks are scored as follows:

- **20 points** for each trick bid and made in diamonds or clubs.
- **30 points** for each trick bid and made in spades and hearts.
- **40 points** for the first trick bid and made in no-trump.
- **30 points** for each additional trick bid and made in no-trump.

To make the scoring clearer, here are some examples:

- If you bid three clubs and won nine tricks, you'd score:
  60 points below the line
- If you bid four spades and won ten tricks, you'd score:
  120 points below the line
- If you bid three no-trump and won nine tricks, you'd score:
  100 points below the line
- If you bid five diamonds and won eleven tricks, you'd score:
  100 points below the line
- If you bid six no-trump and won twelve tricks, you'd score:
  190 points below the line

Game Score

The first partnership to reach 100 points below the line wins **game**.

You may score game by winning one hand or by adding two or more hands together. In order to score game in one hand, you must bid and make the following:

Three no-trump	100 points
Four hearts or four spades	120 points
Five clubs or five diamonds	100 points

You can also win game by adding up the partial scores you have made. For example, if you bid and made two spades, you'd receive 60 points below the line. If, on the next hand, you bid and made two clubs, that would be an additional 40 points below the line, giving you a total of 100 points, which is enough for game. The scoring in this case would look like this:

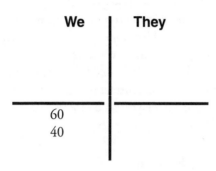

It is also possible to have a partial score and then for your opponents to win game. For example, suppose you bid and made three hearts (for 60 points). Then you bid and made one diamond (for an additional 20 points). You'd now have 80 points. But suppose on the next hand, your opponents (the other partnership), bid and made four spades for 120 points. They'd win game. The scoresheet would look like this:

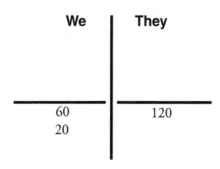

At this point, the game is finished. When all the points are eventually added up, you'll have 80 and your opponents will have 120. For now, another game must be played, and a fresh scoresheet is started.

Winning The Rubber

The first side or partnership to win two games wins the **rubber**. Winning the rubber is important because of the bonus points attached. If you win the rubber two games to none, you score a bonus of 700 points. If you win the rubber two games to one, you score 500 bonus points. All rubber bonus points are scored above the line. As you may recall, I mentioned the term "rubber bridge" at the outset of the book. It gets its name from the rubber, which is the customary unit of play in contract bridge. After a rubber, partners may be changed if the players so desire. Another rubber can also be played with the same partnerships.

Unfinished Rubber

In the event that a rubber cannot be completed, the scoring is as follows:

UNFINISHED RUBBER

One game won	300 points
Partial score	50 points

To review and summarize, here's a chart with all the bonus scoring at the end of bridge play:

RUBBER POINTS

Winning the rubber where opponents have won no game
700 points

Winning the rubber where opponents have won one game
500 points

Unfinished rubber winning one game
300 points

Unfinished rubber for having only part score
50 points

Vulnerability

A side that has scored one game toward rubber is said to be **vulnerable**. If both sides have won a game, then both sides are vulnerable. A side that is vulnerable will be exposed to penalties for failing to fulfill a contract. On the other hand, a vulnerable side will, in most cases, score higher bonus points than a side that is not vulnerable.

Doubled and Redoubled Trick Points

When you make a doubled contract, your trick score is doubled. You will receive the following points:

* **60 points** for each trick bid and made in spades or hearts.
* **40 points** for each trick bid and made in diamonds or clubs.
* **80 points** for the first trick bid and made at no-trump.
* **60 points** for any other trick bid and made at no-trump.

All of these points will be scored below the line, and they will thus count toward game. For example, if you bid and make two spades doubled, your game score below the line would now be 120 points instead of 60, the normal score for two spades bid and made. Bidding and making three clubs doubled will also give you game, since the 60 points for three clubs is now doubled to 120 points. However, bidding and making two diamonds doubled will not give you game—it will give you only 80 points (double 40 points).

When you bid and make a *redoubled* contract, then your score is quadrupled; that is, it's four times the normal value. Thus, if you bid and make one heart, which would ordinarily be worth only 30 points, if your contract is doubled and re-doubled, it now is worth 120 points—good enough for a game score. Any bid in the two level, doubled and redoubled, is a possible game score.

Overtricks

Overtricks are tricks won by the declarer in excess of those necessary to fulfill the contract. For example, if the contract was four spades, which necessitates the winning of ten tricks, and the declarer made eleven tricks, he would have made one overtrick. If the contract was two hearts, which required the winning of eight tricks, and the declarer made ten tricks, he would have made two overtricks.

The scoring for overtricks is the same as for bid and made tricks. The only difference is that overtricks do not count toward game, and they are scored above the line. Let's look at a situation in which you'd have to score overtricks. Let's assume that the bidding on the first hand dealt resulted in a contract of three clubs. As you should be able to determine, the declarer needs to win nine tricks to make this contract. Assume that he instead won eleven tricks. He has given his side two overtricks, since he needed only nine tricks to fulfill his contract. His score would be recorded as follows:

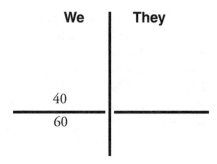

Although the declarer made 100 points in total, his side didn't win a game, since only the bid and made contract of three clubs goes below the line toward game score. The overtricks are scored above the line.

Although they do not count toward game or rubber, above-the-line points are important in their own right. At the end of a bridge session, all points on each side are added up to determine the winning partnership. For example, let's say one side won the rubber and scored 700 points above the line, plus another 240 points for game scores below the line. That side has a total of 940 points.

Meanwhile, let's say the other side scored 1040 total points from successful defense. The side with 1040 total points would actually beat the other partnership by 100 points, even though that partnership won two games. In rubber bridge, all points are important, whether they're scored above or below the line. (See the section on duplicate bridge section for duplicate bridge scoring.)

If the contract was doubled or redoubled, the chart below shows how scores would be awarded, again, above the line. (These scores are standard, whether the contract was played in a major suit, a minor suit, or no-trump.)

POINTS AWARDED
Overtricks (Doubled & Undoubled Contracts)

For Each Overtrick	Not Vulnerable	Vulnerable
Undoubled	Trick Value	Trick Value
Doubled	100	200
Redoubled	200	400

Undertricks

Each trick below the number of tricks necessary to make the contract is an **undertrick**. If the contract was for five clubs, and only eight tricks were made by the declarer, there would be three undertricks.

Not making the contract penalizes the declarer's side, with the penalty points going to the other side, again, above the line.

The following are the penalty points:

PENALTY POINTS
Undertricks (Undoubled Contracts)

	Not Vulnerable	Vulnerable
First Undertrick	50	100
Each Additional Undertrick	50	100

PENALTY POINTS
Undertricks (Doubled Contracts)

	Not Vulnerable	Vulnerable
First Undertrick	100	200
2nd & 3rd Undertrick	200	300
Each Additional Undertrick	300	300

PENALTY POINTS
Undertricks (Redoubled Contracts)

	Not Vulnerable	Vulnerable
First Undertrick	200	400
2nd & 3rd Undertrick	400	600
Each Additional Undertrick	600	600

Honors

Certain high-ranking cards are known as **honors**. If a player holds all the honors—the ace, king, queen, jack and 10 in the trump suit, or all four aces in no-trump, his side receives 150 points. If a player holds any four of the honors in the trump suit, his side receives 100 points.

To summarize:

HONOR POINTS

For holding in one hand:

A K Q J 10 of trump	150 points
Four of the Five trump honors	100 points
All four aces in a no-trump contract	150 points

Any player may receive the honors bonus points, whether he is declarer, dummy or one of the defenders. The usual practice is to announce that you have held the honors at the *end* of play of the hand (so you don't give away the contents of your hand during play). This bonus is given whether the contract was made or set, and whether the side was vulnerable or not vulnerable.

Slams

There are bonuses given for bidding and making twelve tricks, called **small slam**, or all thirteen tricks, called the **grand slam**. Note that the slams must be bid and made. If you bid four hearts and make all thirteen tricks, that's not a grand slam.

The following are the bonus points for slams:

BONUS POINTS FOR SLAMS

	Not Vulnerable	Vulnerable
Small slam	500	750
Grand slam	1000	1500

4. BIDDING BASICS

Introduction

Bidding allows the partners to exchange information and to glean information from the bids of the opposing partnership. Sometimes one side dominates the bidding on a particular hand, and the players learn nothing from the other partnership, which becomes the defense. For example, look at the following bidding sequence:

SOUTH	WEST	NORTH	EAST
1 spade	Pass	2 spades	Pass
4 spades	Pass	Pass	Pass

All that the declaring side of South and North have learned from the bidding is that West and East are too weak to put in any kind of opening bid. All that the defenders have gleaned is that spades was bid, and nothing else. In this case, very little information passed between the partnerships.

From the little I've told you about bidding, you might now be asking yourself: what kind of hand is strong enough to bid on? How do I analyze my hand to open the bidding, and if my partner has bid, how do I respond?

These are important questions in bridge. Whether you open the bidding or respond to your partner's bid, you want to convey information about your hand to your partner. Why do you want to do this? So that you and your partner can arrive at the correct contract and win the maximum number of points from your combined hands. To do this, you must know which suit to choose as trump, or whether to play the hand in no-trump.

The defenders also want to give information to each other during the bidding, but often the weakness of their hands precludes them from putting in any kind of bid. Since the defenders lead first, they must pay strict attention to the other side's bidding. It will help them know which suit and card to lead.

Without knowing the value of your hand, you'd be playing a guessing game, so the first step in correct bidding is to value your hand. I'll teach you how to do that now.

Valuing The Hand

There are several methods to help you value your hand, but the most important one is the point count popularized by Charles Goren many decades ago. It is still valid and is the standard in contract bridge. It's based on the high cards in the hand, along with the **short suits**—suits in which you hold just one or two cards, or suits in which you are void.

The Point Count

Practically all bridge players are familiar with this count, so if you want to be able to play with any partner, you should know it. Besides being popular, it is a correct way to evaluate and value a hand.

The first step is to determine your hand's high-card point value, which you do according to the following table:

Each ace	4 points
Each king	3 points
Each queen	2 points
Each jack	1 point

Next, you should examine the short suits and value them:

Void suit - no cards in a suit	3 points
Singleton - one card in a suit	2 points
Doubleton - two cards in a suit	1 point

The above points are valid only for hands in which there is a trump suit. With no-trump hands, the short suit values aren't counted; just the high card points. If you disregard the short suit points (also called **distribution points**) you can readily see that there are only forty high card points in the entire deck.

Let's examine a few hands and determine how many points we have:

♠ A Q J 5 3   ♥ K J 8 2   ♦ K 9 3   ♣ 5

In this hand we have fourteen points in high cards and two in short suits (the club singleton), for a total of sixteen points. Let's look at another:

♠ K 8 4   ♥ J 9 6   ♦ A K Q 3 2   ♣ 9 4

In this hand we have thirteen points in high cards and one in the short suit (the club doubleton) for a total of fourteen points. If we were to evaluate the hand as a no-trump hand, it would contain just thirteen high card points. As I've said, short suits do not help no-trump hands. You'll see why that's true in a later section.

Sometimes you cannot value a hand easily despite the point count. For example, if you have a singleton king, it can be lost to an opponent's ace, and therefore cannot be given full value as a high card. It should be reduced from three to two points. As a singleton, it will still receive two points as a short suit. Therefore, a singleton king should be valued at four points.

If you have a singleton queen, then its high point value should be reduced from two to one, with two points for the singleton as a short suit. A jack, however, will yield no high card points as a singleton; it will receive just the two points as a short suited card.

Aces are very important and powerful, since they command suits as the highest ranking card. A hand without an ace but with other high

CARDOZA PUBLISHING • PLAY BRIDGE NOW!

card points should therefore be reduced by one point. Conversely, a hand containing three or four aces could be increased by one point.

Points Necessary for Game

To refresh your memory, game consists of four of a major suit bid and made (120 points), or five of a minor suit bid and made (100 points). In no-trump contracts, three no-trump has to be bid and made (100 points). Generally speaking, a total of twenty-six (26) high and distributional points together in both partnership hands is necessary to bid and make a game in major suits. A total of twenty-nine (29) points is generally necessary for game in the minor suits. In no-trump, only honor or high card points are counted.

If the parnership has less than these total points, it will usually have to settle for a partial score rather than a game score. For example, the partnership might have to settle for a contract of three spades or four diamonds, which, if made, will result in a partial, not a game score.

Points Necessary for Slam

A small slam is six of any suit or no-trump bid and made. A grand slam is seven of any suit or no-trump bid and made. Thirty-three (33) points are generally necessary for a small slam, and thirty-seven (37) points are generally necessary for a grand slam.

The above point totals don't guarantee that you can make the hand. They are good guidelines for game and slam bidding, but other factors may enter into the situation, such as how well your hand fits with your partner's hand, or the distribution of cards in a particular suit in a defender's hand. Sometimes, if everything fits, you can reach game with only twenty-four (24) or twenty-five (25) points, but don't reach too far with too few points. That's the way to invite disaster (contracts that are set).

Let's now examine the factors that will determine whether you will make an opening bid and what your bid will be.

5. OPENING THE BIDDING

An **opening bid** is the first bid made in a suit or in no-trump. If West was the dealer and passed, then North passed, and East bid one spade, East's bid would be the opening bid. A pass is not considered an opening bid.

Opening Suit Bids at the One Level
There are several considerations that must be examined to determine whether you can open the bidding in a suit at the one-level—that is, bid either one club, one diamond, one heart or one spade.

Biddable Suits
The general rule is that any five-card or longer suit is biddable. In modern practice, many players require five cards in a major suit to bid at the one-level, but some players might still bid a four-card major suit. The reason that five-card suits are preferable has to do with the rebidding by the opening bidder. A rebiddable suit is one which may be bid a second time. A four-card suit is not rebiddable in most cases, and since players prefer to play out hands in major suits because of the difference in scoring, it may be difficult to reach the correct contract if you open a four-card major suit.

The exception is when you open a four-card major suit, such as spades, and your partner responds in spades, showing strength in the same suit. Then the four-card major may be rebid. But if the response is in a minor suit, the opener may be in a quandary, unless he has strength in another major suit. Let's look at a hand to illustrate this point. You hold the following:

♠ A K 6 4   ♥ A Q 9 5   ♦ 8 7   ♣ 9 4 3

The hand contains thirteen high card points and an additional point for the doubleton in diamonds, for a total of fourteen points. You open with one spade, and your partner responds with two diamonds. You can now bid your heart suit and give your partner the choice of rebidding spades. If your partner had responded to your one spade bid with a bid of two hearts, then you'd know that hearts was the best suit for trump. You could raise to three hearts and play the hand at that contract.

I said that five-card suits can be bid as opening one-level suit bids. I should also add that any five-card suit must be headed by at least a 10, while a four-card suit should have at least a Q J (or stronger cards) heading it. A king and 10 heading a four-card suit is acceptable. Thus, the following suits are biddable:

♣ K 10 8 7

♣ J 9 5 4 2

♠ A 10 9 5 4

And the following suit—a weak four-card major headed only by a jack—is not:

♥ J 7 5 2

Point Requirements to Open One in a Suit

In order to open the bidding at the one-level in a suit, you should have at least thirteen points. But sometimes, even with thirteen points (high-card plus distributional points) it is difficult to find an opening bid because you have no biddable suit. Let's look at this situation in the following hand:

♠ 10 9 5 4 ♥ A Q 2 ♦ A Q 4 ♣ J 8 6

Here you have a hand containing thirteen honor points, but you have no good opening bid. Your spade suit has no honors—it's only a weak four-card suit. Your other suits have only three cards. If, however, your cards were slightly different, you could have a correct opening bid.

♠ 9 4   ♥ A Q 10 5 2   ♦ A Q 4   ♣ J 8 6

Now you could open with one heart. You have a five-card major suit headed by A Q, the same thirteen honor points, and one additional point for distribution (the spade doubleton).

Let's look at another slightly different hand:

♠ 9 5 4   ♥ A Q 6   ♦ A Q 10 4   ♣ J 8 6

You cannot bid the major suits—spades and hearts—since you have only three of each suit. Your diamond suit, however, is now of sufficient length for you to make an opening bid of one diamond. In a minor suit, only four cards are necessary for an opening bid, provided that your suit is headed by sufficient honors, as it is in this case. You have thirteen points in high cards and a biddable diamond suit.

With fourteen points in honors and in distributional points, you must make an opening bid. Bridge is a competitive game. If possible, you want to get in an opening bid—you'd rather be in charge of the bidding than have your opponents get control. Thus, with a biddable suit and thirteen points, you *should* bid at the one-suit level. With fourteen points, you absolutely *must* make that first opening bid.

Let's look at another hand:

♠ 6   ♥ A 10 5   ♦ K Q 9 3 2   ♣ 9 7 5

The above hand contains twelve points in honors, plus two distributional points for the spade singleton, for a total of fourteen points. The heart suit contains only three cards and is not biddable. The diamond suit, however, stands out with five cards headed by two honors. The logical bid here is one diamond.

You may make opening bids with hands containing twelve points, as long as your bid suit is fairly strong—has two honors and a length of five or six cards. A good time to bid a hand weaker than thirteen points is in third position, when your partner has not opened. Your opening bid here might disrupt the last opposing player's potential opening bid. For example, if you hold twelve points with a biddable suit and there have been two passes to you, you can venture an opening bid.

If you hold less than twelve points in distribution and high card points, don't open the bidding. Even if you are in the fourth seat and there have been three passes to you, you're only asking for trouble and a penalty if you open the bidding with a hand containing ten or eleven points. Your partner has already passed, which tells you he also has a weak hand.

Opening No-Trump Bids
The One No-Trump Opening Bid
No-trump is the fastest way to make game in rubber bridge. It takes only nine tricks (three no-trump bid and made) for game in no-trump, whereas it takes ten tricks bid and made in the major suits and eleven tricks bid and made in the minor suits. Just because it's the fastest way to game doesn't mean that you should take shortcuts and switch to no-trump whenever you feel like it.

No-trump contracts require certain high card strengths and balanced distribution. If you overlook these two factors, you and your partner are headed for trouble.

HIGH CARD POINTS NECESSARY

Here are the necessary high card points for various contracts in no-trump:

- **Twenty-six (26) points**
  ...will usually be sufficient for a three no-trump game.
- **Thirty-three (33) points**
  ...will usually be sufficient for a six no-trump game.
- **Thirty-seven (37) points**
  ...will usually be sufficient for a seven no-trump game.

Keep the above numbers in mind when you're bidding on a no-trump contract.

Here are the requirements for opening bids of one in no-trump:

REQUIREMENTS: OPENING BID 1 NO-TRUMP

- 16-18 high card points (distributional points do not count in no-trump contracts).
- Balanced distribution in suits (4-3-3-3 is the best, then 4-4-3-2, then 5-3-3-2).
- All suits stopped (at least one honor covering each suit).

To help you better understand what I mean by "stopped suits," here's a hand with examples of protected and stopped suits ("x" represents a small or irrelevant card, such as 8, 6 or 2):

$$\spadesuit A x x \quad \heartsuit K x \quad \diamondsuit Q x x x \quad \clubsuit J x x x$$

The ace, even as a singleton, will win a trick and stop a suit. The king needs another card with it for protection. The queen needs two other cards, and the jack needs three other cards to be able to stop a suit.

Here are some things to keep in mind when bidding no-trump contracts:

1. Your short suit is usually your opponent's long suit. You must guard against the possibility of an opponent establishing his long suit and cashing in tricks (winning tricks).

2. Avoid bidding no-trump contracts when you have a void or a singleton. Glance back now at the necessary distribution outlined above.

3. It is necessary to protect suits with stoppers. A stopper is any card that can prevent the opponents from running a suit (cashing in a number of tricks). The ideal stopper is the ace. Since the game is played without trumps, the ace is a sure winner of a trick. Another sure stopper would be the king and queen of a suit. Even if one honor falls to an opponent's ace, the other will win a trick.

A king with a small card may be a stopper, and the same holds true for a queen with two small cards or a jack with three small cards. You can use these to bid no-trump contracts, since they are all probable stoppers. Even stronger than holding a queen with two small cards is holding the queen and jack in a suit. Also strong is the combination of jack-10-9-8 of a suit. If you have no probable stopper in one suit, avoid bidding no-trump.

4. Don't fudge on the high card point count. Don't stretch one no-trump opening bids with fewer than sixteen points. When you open one no-trump, your partner should expect that you have 16-18 points—period!

You now know that 13-15 points means you should open at the one level, and 16-18 points means you should bid one no-trump. What if you have even more points? Should you still open by bidding just one of a suit or no-trump? Not exactly. With 19-21 high card points and balanced distribution, you should still open with one of a suit. Then you should make a jump bid in no-trump after your partner responds.

With even more points, you should again be opening in no-trump, but this time at the two or three level. Let's take a more detailed look at what these bids require. The following are the requirements for an opening bid of two no-trump:

> • 22-24 high card points
> • Balanced distribution
> • All four suits protected

If you open two no-trump, you can't assume that your partner will definitely reply. As you'll learn in the chapter on responding, a two no-trump bid is not a forcing bid—it does not require a response from your partner.

The following are the requirements for an opening bid of three no-trump:

> • 25-27 high points
> • Balanced distribution
> • All four suits protected

Let's examine some hands to see what the correct bid should be. Suppose you are dealt the following:

♠ A 5 4   ♥ K 9 3   ♦ Q J 10   ♣ A K J 5

You have eighteen high card points and balanced distribution. There are stoppers in all suits. Bid one no-trump.

♠ K Q 9　♥ A K J　♦ K Q 8 3　♣ A J 6

You have twenty-three points in high cards, balanced distribution, and stoppers in all suits. Bid two no-trump.

♠ K Q 8　♥ A K J　♦ A K J　♣ K Q J 5

This hand contains twenty-seven high card points, stoppers in every suit, and perfect distribution of 3-3-3-4. Open the bidding with three no-trump.

Short-Club Bid

If you and your partner decide to bid only five-card major suits, the short-club convention is another good choice for an opening bid. It's an artificial bid—that is, the bid doesn't show strength in the suit you've bid; it's made for convenience.

Here's how it works. Suppose you hold the following cards:

♠ K Q 8 3　♥ A 9 7 2　♦ A J　♣ 8 7 6

You have fourteen points in high cards, and therefore you want to make an opening suit bid. However, both your major suits are only four cards in length, and you bid only five-card majors. What do you do? If you and your partner have agreed on the short-club convention, you open with one club.

You now wait for your partner's response. You are telling him that you hold no five-card major biddable suit.

If he responds with one of the major suits, then you know that will be the correct suit for the contract.

Opening Bids of Two in a Suit*

Opening the bidding with two in a suit, such as two diamonds or two spades, shows a very powerful hand, good enough to go to game by itself. It is a forcing bid, demanding that the partnership go at least to game contract. When a player has such a strong hand, it is important that he open the bidding at the two-level, since his partner, if she holds less than six points, can pass an opening bid of a suit in the one-level.

Not only must his partner respond to the opening two-bid, but she must keep responding until at least game contract is reached. That's how strong the hand is that is opened in a suit at the two-level.

The following are the requirements for opening in a suit at the two-level:

- **Twenty-five points**—both high cards and distributional strength—with a good five-card suit. (If you hold two good five-card suits, you need only twenty-four points.)
- **Twenty-three points** with a good six-card suit. A good suit is a strong suit, headed by a couple of high honors.
- **Twenty-one points** with a good seven-card suit.

If you'll be playing the hand in a minor suit, two more points must be added to the above requirements. For example, if you held a good six-card suit in diamonds, you'd need twenty-five, instead of the twenty-three points necessary if your strong suit was a major, such as spades. The reason for this rule is that making game in a minor suit requires that you win eleven tricks rather than the ten you need to fulfill a major suit game.

*There are two different conventions for opening the bidding with two in a suit, called "weak twos" and "strong twos." I will be teaching only the strong twos convention in this book.

Let's now examine some hands:

♠ 9 ♥ K Q J 10 4 ♦ A K Q 5 ♣ A K J

Your correct bid is two hearts. You have a solid five-card major, twenty-three points in high cards, and, with the additional two points for the spade singleton, a total of twenty-five points.

♠ A Q J 9 5 4 ♥ K Q 4 ♦ A K Q ♣ 8

Bid two spades. You have a solid six-card major suit and twenty-one points in high cards, plus two points for the singleton club. You fill the requirements of twenty-three points and a good six-card major.

♠ A K Q 10 8 5 3 ♥ A Q 6 ♦ A 7 ♣ 2

Bid two spades. You have nineteen points in high cards, plus three additional points in distribution (2 for the club singleton and 1 for the diamond doubleton). Plus you have an outstanding seven-card major suit. Your twenty-two points exceeds the requirement of twenty-one points with a good seven-card major.

♠ K Q 5 ♥ A K Q ♦ A K Q 9 4 2 ♣ 5

Bid two diamonds. Since you're in a minor suit, you need twenty-five instead of twenty-three points to open at the two-level. You have twenty-three points in high cards, plus two more in distribution for the club singleton, which gives you the necessary twenty-five points. Once again, the reason that you need two more points in a minor suit is that game there is eleven tricks, not ten.

Pre-emptive or Shut-out Bid

An opening bid of three, four or five in a suit is a **pre-emptive** or **shut-out bid**. These bids are made with hands that are relatively weak in high-card points, and their primary purpose is to destroy the line of communication of the opponents. The pre-emptive bidder fears that the opponents have powerful hands, and if left unimpeded, their bidding might even take them to slam level. By throwing in the pre-emptive bid, he hopes to force the opponents either to overbid their hands at high levels or to bid inaccurately (also at high levels).

There is a danger in making a pre-emptive bid. The bidder may be doubled by the opponents, and then be set by several tricks, with many penalty points going to the other side. That is the basic negative of a pre-emptive bid. It must be weighed in those terms: how many points will the bidder be penalized versus how many points has he saved his side by preventing the other partnership from bidding and making a slam.

There are two constants of the pre-emptive bidder's hand: it will be lacking in high cards, and it will contain a long suit. Most experts agree that you should never make a pre-emptive bid with a hand containing more than nine points in high cards when you're not vulnerable, nor with a hand containing more than ten points in high cards when you are vulnerable.

This is known as the "safety" factor. A player making a shut-out bid must be prepared to be doubled and lose points. However, he should limit his losses to 500 points at the most. This means he may overbid by three tricks when not vulnerable, and by two tricks when vulnerable. In either event, the loss is 500 points.

When you make a pre-emptive bid, you are assuming that you will be doubled, that you will go down a number of tricks, and that your partner has absolutely nothing to help your hand. You figure you'll win only those tricks you see in your hand.

Here's a good way to figure out the potential tricks you need:

- With an opening bid of three in a suit, you need to win in your hand six tricks when not vulnerable, and seven tricks when vulnerable. To put that another way, you can afford to go down three tricks when not vulnerable, and only two tricks when vulnerable.

- With an opening bid of four in a suit, you need to win seven tricks from your hand when not vulnerable and eight tricks when vulnerable.

- With an opening bid of five in a suit, you must win eight tricks from your hand when not vulnerable and nine when vulnerable.

Here are some examples of hands with which you could make a pre-emptive bid ("x" again represents an irrelevant low card, such as a 2-8):

♠ K Q J x x x x x   ♥ x   ♦ x x   ♣ x x

If you're not vulnerable, the correct pre-emptive bid with this hand is four spades. If you are vulnerable, bid only three spades. Four spades, not vulnerable, is an overbid of three tricks. Three spades, vulnerable, is an overbid of two tricks. In either event, if you get doubled, the loss is 500 points.

♠ x   ♥ Q J 10 9   ♦ x   ♣ Q J 10 9 x x x

Your hand can win five club tricks and two heart tricks. Your bid would be four clubs if not vulnerable, three clubs if vulnerable.

When you make a pre-emptive bid, you must realize you are sacrificing yourself and being penalized. More often than not, though, you'll be disrupting the opponents and saving points in the long run by preventing them from bidding and making slam contracts.

Summary

In essence, when you open the bidding (other than with a pre-emptive bid), you are beginning a dialogue with your partner. Between his responses and your rebids, you are attempting to find the correct contract. A correct contract is the highest possible bid that can be made. For example, if you and your partner arrive at a final contract of three spades, which is scored as 90 points, but in the course of play you won ten tricks (enough for four spades) then your bidding was incorrect. Instead of reaching game with 120 points, you received only 90 points below the line and 30 above the line for the overtrick.

If your final bid was four spades but you were able to win only nine tricks (and you were therefore set in the contract) again your bidding was wrong. What you must endeavor to do is bid a final contract that you will make with the exact number of tricks. That's easier said than done, of course, and failing to make a contract will not always be your fault. The distribution of trump cards in your opponents' hands might be uneven.

Suppose as declarer you hold five spades and the dummy shows three, for a total of eight. Ideally, as we shall see in the section on playing out of the hand, you want the remaining trump to be split 3-2 on the other side. If it is split at 5-0, that's a bad break for you and may jeopardize the making of your contract. These things happen. Bridge is a game of skill, but luck does enter into it.

6. RESPONDING TO AN OPENER

Up to this point, we've assumed you were the opener. But now, sitting at the bridge table opposite your partner, you find that she has opened the bidding. At this point, you are the **responder**. Your response is important—it will show your partner the strength of your hand, and in what suits you have that strength. Thus, your partner, who opened the bidding, will be able to rebid correctly, and you'll be on your way to finding the ideal and correct contract in which to play the hand.

Responses to Opening Suit Bids of One

When you're responding to an opening bid of one in a suit, you have several options open to you. We'll assume that the intervening player has passed, so that after your partner's first bid, your response will now be the next bid. Let's now discuss your options.

Unless you have at least six points in high cards in your hand, you should pass. There's a good reason for this rule. With fewer than six points in your hand, you have a very weak hand, and you won't be able to help your partner. No matter how tempted you are to throw in a bid, a pass is in order. In the long run, it will save you from disastrous contracts and penalty points awarded to your opponents.

The following is a typical weak hand:

♠ J 6 3   ♥ 8 4 3 2   ♦ K 6 2   ♣ J 8 4

You have only five high-card points, with no long suit and no doubleton or singleton, which would be of use to your partner. Pass.

A Raise of One Over One

A raise of **one over one** means a response at the same level as the opening bid in a suit. For example, suppose your partner bid one diamond. By bidding one heart or one spade, you're staying at the same one-level. (We'll discuss a response of one-no trump in a later section; it is a special response.)

Suppose your partner opened with one heart, and you responded with two clubs. That's no longer a one over one response. Two clubs is in the two level. If you had responded instead with one spade, it would still be a one over one response.

The following diagram shows the bidding sequence for a one over one response. You are North; your partner is South.

SOUTH	WEST	NORTH	EAST
1 Diamond	Pass	1 Spade	

Your response of one spade is a typical one over one bid.

A one over one response is not a weak bid; rather it is a **forcing bid**. By "forcing", I mean that it strategically forces the opener to bid again for at least one more round in order to ensure that the partnership arrives at the best contract.

When I mention *forcing*, it is always in the strategic sense, not as a law at bridge itself. Therefore, after responding one over one, you should expect your partner to rebid her hand. If, however, there is an intervening bid by an opponent, the opener is no longer required (or forced) to bid again. Below is an example of an intervening bid by the other side. Again, you and your partner are sitting North and South, with your partner, the dealer, making the first bid.

SOUTH	WEST	NORTH	EAST
1 Diamond	Pass	1 Spade	2 Hearts

East's bid of two hearts is an intervening bid, and now South is no longer forced to rebid. She is not precluded from bidding—she may certainly bid again if her hand is strong—but she is no longer forced to rebid.

Requirements for Responding One over One

Your partner has opened with a suit bid at the one level. The following requirements are necessary for your response of one over one:

- Four or more cards in the bid suit.
- 6 to 17 points.

When you make a response bid of one over one, the four-card suit you bid doesn't have to headed by an honor. All you need is a four-card suit. Let's examine the next hand. You are holding these cards:

♠ K 6   ♥ 10 9 8 4   ♦ Q J 7   ♣ J 9 8 5

Your partner has opened with one diamond. You are holding seven points in high cards and two four-card suits. If you respond in hearts, you keep the bidding at the one-level. You also respond in a major suit. When you're faced with a choice to respond in a major suit or a minor suit with a hand like this, the major suit is always preferable.

Suppose that instead of clubs, your other four-card suit was spades, and thus, you had a choice of responding in either major suit. In this situation, respond in the lower of the two: hearts.

The One No-Trump Response

This response is often used just to keep the bidding open. Suppose you want to keep the bidding alive, but you find that you have no suit that you can bid at the one-level, for a one over one response. You also find that you have six or more honor points in your hand. You should think about a one no-trump response.

Here's what you need to respond one no-trump:

- 6 to 10 honor points (remember that when you bid no-trump, distributional points do not count).
- No biddable suit at the one level.

Let's now look at some hands to see how this bid works.

♠ J 9 4   ♥ 7 4   ♦ Q 9 6 2   ♣ A J 6 5

Your partner has opened with one heart. You have no biddable suit at the one-level. You have only three spades, and a diamond or club bid moves you into the second level of bidding. You have eight high-card points, so you can't afford to pass—you want to keep the bidding alive. You should therefore bid one no-trump.

Here's another hand:

♠ K 6   ♥ 4 3   ♦ A 8 6 3 2   ♣ J 8 5 4

Again, your partner has opened with one heart. You have eight honor points and cannot bid a suit in the one-level (to bid diamonds would require that you bid at the two-level). A one no-trump response will keep the bidding alive.

In the next instance, your partner has opened with one spade, and you hold the following hand:

♠ 9 5 4   ♥ K 9 5 2   ♦ Q 10 8   ♣ J 5 3

You have eight high-card points and want to keep the bidding alive; bid one no-trump. Remember, with a one no-trump response, you are being very specific in limiting the honor strength of your hand. It will contain not less than six points and no more than ten points.

The response of one no-trump is not forcing, since the opener can ascertain the outer limits of his honor strength. If he has thirteen points in his hand, he now knows that the most the partnership will have is twenty-three points, and possibly only nineteen—certainly not enough for game. To refresh your memory, you need twenty-six points for game.

Single Raise of Opener's Suit

This is also a non-forcing bid, which means that the opener need not rebid his hand. A single raise is just what its name implies: a bid one higher than the opening bid in the same suit. For example, if the opening bid was one diamond, a two diamond response would be a single raise.

Like the one no-trump response to an opening bid, a single raise is very specific in its limits. The following is necessary for a single raise in the opener's bid suit:

- 7-10 points
- A minimum of three cards in the suit if a major suit was bid, or of four cards in the suit if a minor suit was bid.

Since most players open with a five-card major, the single raise will then assure the opener that the partnership has a fit of at least eight trumps. However, if the opener bid a minor suit, he may have only four (or even three) cards in the suit. He will then know that the responder has at least four more trumps in his hand in the minor suit.

Note that, unlike the one no-trump response, for which six *honor* points were required, the 7-10 points required for a single raise can come from both honor points and distributional values.

Let's now look at some representative hands. Your partner has opened with one spade, and you hold the following hand:

♠ K 9 5 4   ♥ 9 5   ♦ J 7 6 2   ♣ Q 8 3

Respond with two spades. You have good trump support and seven points—six in honors and one for the heart singleton.

In the next hand, your partner has opened with one heart. You hold the following:

♠ Q 8   ♥ 9 6 2   ♦ 10 8 5 3   ♣ Q 8 7 5

Your correct bid is to pass. You have only four honor points plus an extra point for the spade doubleton. That's two below the seven required for the single raise. Your hand is quite weak, with little support for your partner.

Let's look at one final hand. Your partner has opened one heart and you hold the following cards:

♠ 5 4   ♥ Q 9 3   ♦ A 9 5 2   ♣ 9 7 6 3

Your correct bid is two hearts. It's a minimum raise, though, when you have just six honor points, a distribution point for the doubleton spade, and only three hearts.

One final note: *Remember that the single raise should not be made with more than ten points.* It is limited to a range of 7-10 points, and it's not forcing.

Two Over One Response

A two over one response means that you name a new suit at the two-level. The suit you are bidding is lower ranking than the suit your partner has opened. For example, suppose your partner opened the bidding with one heart. If you had a good spade suit and the requisite points, you could still stay in the one-level with a response of one spade, a one over one response. Therefore, two spades would not be a two over one response. It would be known as a **jump response**, and we'll get to those in a moment.

Let's go back to your partner's bid of one heart. To make a two over one response, you would have to bid one of the minor suits at the two-level. If your partner had opened with one spade, a two-bid in any of the other suits would be a two over one response.

A response of two over one is forcing for one round. This means that your partner must rebid his hand; he is strategically forced to do so by your response.

Here are the requirements for a two over one response:

- A good suit, with five or more cards.
- At least 10 points in honors.
- 10-18 points, counting distributional strength.

Suppose your partner opened with one spade. You hold the following cards:

$$\spadesuit 864 \quad \heartsuit A5 \quad \diamondsuit KQJ93 \quad \clubsuit 852$$

You hold ten honor points, plus an additional point for the doubleton in hearts. You also have a solid five-card suit in diamonds. Your correct bid would be two diamonds, a two over one response. Let's examine some other hands.

Your partner has opened with one heart, and you hold the following:

$$\spadesuit 85 \quad \heartsuit 32 \quad \diamondsuit J543 \quad \clubsuit AKQ84$$

Bid two clubs. You have ten honor points and two doubletons, a total of twelve points. You also have a strong five-card club suit.

Generally speaking, the two over one response is treated by experts as a decisive step towards a game contract. Let's go back to a previous hand to see how this process works. You hold:

$$\spadesuit\,864 \quad \heartsuit\,A5 \quad \diamondsuit\,KQJ93 \quad \clubsuit\,852$$

Your partner opened with one spade, and you correctly responded with two diamonds. Now you can bid further. Let's assume that your partner now rebid her spades, still at the two level. You can raise to three spades, since the ideal contract seems to lie in spades. Between you, you have at least eight spades, assuming your partner opened with a five-card major. If she believes the combined point-count is enough, she might bid four spades, thus giving your partnership a chance to make game.

In the next example, your partner has opened with one heart. You hold the following hand:

$$\spadesuit\,9 \quad \heartsuit\,9653 \quad \diamondsuit\,AKQ54 \quad \clubsuit\,Q82$$

Your correct response here is two diamonds. If your partner rebids her hearts you can raise in hearts, showing support with your four-card suit.

No-Trump Responses

So far, we've examined only the one no-trump response to an opening bid of one in a suit. To remind you, a one no-trump response showed 6-10 honor points (distribution points aren't counted in no-trump responses) and no biddable suit at the one level. Basically, a one no-trump response to an opening bid of one in a suit is a weak bid.

Let's now take a moment to discuss the requirements for other no-trump responses.

A two no-trump response shows the following:

- 13-15 points in high cards.
- Strength in each of the unbid suits. (If your partner opened with one heart, this means you will have strength in clubs, diamonds and spades).
- Balanced distribution.

In no-trump contracts, short suits are detrimental to the playing of the hand. They easily are depleted during the playing of the hand, and opponents may then run the rest of the suit as winners. Since there are no trumps available, once you're void in a suit, the opponents have control if they lead that suit. It's therefore essential that you have balanced distribution—you don't want to have a singleton or a void suit.

Let's now look at a few hands. Your partner has opened with one heart and you hold the following hand:

♠ K J 5 ♥ 8 3 ♦ A Q 8 3 ♣ K J 7 6

You should bid two no-trump. You hold fourteen points in high cards (honors) and you have strength in all the suits except hearts, which was bid by your partner. Also your distribution, though not perfect, is balanced at 3-2-4-4. (An ideal distribution for no-trump contracts is 4-3-3-3.)

Here's another hand. Your partner has opened with one spade. You hold the following cards:

♠ 9 4 ♥ Q 10 6 ♦ A Q 8 5 ♣ K Q 9 3

Bid two no-trump. You hold thirteen high-card points, with strength in all the unbid suits, and a balanced distribution.

A three no-trump response shows the following:

- 16-17 points in high cards.
- Strength in each of the unbid suits.
- Balanced distribution, preferably a distribution of 4-3-3-3.

Here's a hand that should be bid at three no-trump following a partner's opening bid of one spade:

$$♠ J 7 5 \quad ♥ K Q 6 \quad ♦ K Q 5 \quad ♣ K Q 8 5$$

This hand contains sixteen high card points, strength in all the unbid suits, and a perfect 3-3-3-4 distribution.

Jump Raises by Responder

A **jump raise** is one that is a level above the possible response. This is a strong response, promising a hand that is fairly powerful. For example, if the opening bid was one spade, a jump raise would be three spades. That's a jump over the possible two spade response. When someone makes such a bid, it is called a jump raise in opener's bid suit (spade-spade). When the jump response to a one heart opening bid, for example, is two spades, that's known as a jump response in a new suit, or a **jump-shift**. That kind of jump response is more powerful than simply jump raising in the opener's suit; we'll get to it in a moment.

For a jump response in the opener's suit, the requirements are:

- 13-16 points.
- At least four of the trump suit (suit bid), headed by at least a queen.

As you may recall, you need twenty-six points for game, and since the opener is presumed to have at least thirteen points, the jump response is telling the opener that game is possible, and it is considered as a bid forcing to game. The more trumps you hold, the higher you can bid, especially in a major suit.

Major Suit Raises

When your partner opens the bidding with one in a major suit, you can raise her in that bid suit if you have sufficient trump support and enough card strength. The following list shows the points you need (high cards plus distributional points) for various raises, as well as the minimum trump strength.

• For a *raise from 1 to 2* (e.g. the opener has bid one spade and you respond with two spades), you need 7-10 points and three or four trumps. If you're holding just three trumps, it's preferable to have your suit led by at least a queen.

• For a *raise from 1 to 3*, you need 13-16 points and four trumps, headed by at least a queen.

• For a *raise from 1 to 4*, you need only 7-10 points, but you must have five of the bid suit.

As I mentioned before, the higher you raise, the more trumps you must have. When you bid four, you stop the bidding, telling your partner in essence, "end the bidding; play the hand in four spades." A raise to four in the suit is known as a **shutout bid**. It stops the bidding by this partnership. With a bid of three spades, you're keeping the bidding alive.

The rules above may seem a little complicated at first, but once you have some experience at the bridge table, they'll become clearer. What is important is to arrive at a bid that best reflects the partnership's hands and is the highest bid possible, because the higher the bid, the more points are scored. This is especially true in duplicate bridge, where your partnership is playing against many other partnerships, and each hand must be bid and made to the fullest limit to score winning points.

Jump Response in a New Suit

A jump response is not only forcing to game, it also carries with it the suggestion that the bidding might go all the way to slam. The following are the requirements for a jump response in a new suit:

- 19 points or more, both in high cards and in distributional values.
- A solid suit or good support for opener's bid suit.

Let's look at some hands now. In the first example your partner has opened with one diamond. You hold:

$$\spadesuit K 8 \quad \heartsuit A K J 9 6 \quad \diamondsuit K Q 8 6 \quad \clubsuit K 10$$

Your correct bid in this instance is two hearts. By making a jump response in a new suit, you're promising your partner at least nineteen points, which you have in high cards alone. After your partner re-bids, you can show your support in her diamond suit.

Your partner in the next example has opened with one heart. You hold the following cards:

$$\spadesuit A Q J 8 4 \quad \heartsuit K Q 9 6 \quad \diamondsuit 7 \quad \clubsuit K Q 3$$

Bid two spades here. Your jump response in a new suit shows that you have nineteen points. When you rebid your heart suit, you will tell your partner that you also have strong support for his heart suit.

Thus far we've dealt with opening bids of one in a suit and the various responses to those bid.

Now we'll look at responses to opening bids of one no-trump.

Responses to Opening No-Trump Bids

Whenever your partner opens the bidding in no-trump, you know the parameters of his bid in high-card points. If he opened with one no-trump, you know that he holds 16-18 points. If he opened two no-trump, he has 22-24 points. With a three no-trump opening bid, he is holding 25-27 points in high cards or honors. It's much easier to know the strength of an opener bidding in no-trump than in a suit because the boundaries of his high card strength are more apparent.

You need to know how to respond to all of these bids; let's first look at how to respond to a one no-trump opener.

Responses to Opening Bids of One No-Trump

You must not forget that you need twenty-six points to make game at three no-trump. Also, you must examine your hand to see if it is balanced or unbalanced as to distribution. A balanced hand could be one in which the distribution is 5-3-3-2, with the five card suit a minor suit. Of course, as you know, other acceptable distributions for no-trump are 4-3-3-3 or 4-4-3-2.

- If you hold **0-7 points**, you are interested in a partial score (below 100 points).
- If you hold **8-9 points**, you are also interested in a partial score.
- If you hold **10-14 points**, you want a game score (three no-trump).
- With **15-16 points**, you're thinking of slam.
- With **17 or more points**, you will bid for a slam.

Remember, you need twenty-six points for game, thirty-three points for a small slam (six no-trump) and thirty-seven points for a grand slam (seven no-trump). Again, when we discuss points here, we're talking about high card points; distributional points play no role in no-trump bidding.

Knowing this, here's what to do with your point totals:

• **0-7 points** - Pass. Satisfy yourself with a partial score. Why? Because 7 plus partner's 18 points (at best; he may be holding 16 points) don't add up to game.

• **8-9 points** - Raise to two no-trump.

• **10-14 points** - Raise to three no-trump.

• **15-16 points** - Raise to four no-trump.

• **17-18 points** - Raise to six no-trump, a small slam bid.

• **19-20 points** - Think of a grand slam. Some experts advise not directly bidding six no-trump here, but first making a jump-shift to three in a suit, then following up with a bid of six no-trump. They consider it stronger than just bidding six no-trump.

• **21 or more points** - Bid the grand slam of seven no-trump. Even if your partner has only sixteen points, you're assured of at least thirty-seven points combined. Since there are only forty high-card points in the deck, and an ace is worth four honor points, your opponents aren't holding an ace when your partnership has a combined thirty-seven points.

The Stayman Convention

Popularized by Samuel Stayman, this convention is accepted by bridge players worldwide. In a nutshell, the **Stayman Convention** calls for a response of two clubs to a one no-trump opener, asking the opener to bid a four-card major. If the opener doesn't have a four-card major, his automatic rebid is two diamonds. Both the two club and two diamond bids are artificial—that is, they don't show strength in those minor suits when bid as part of the Stayman Convention. If the original bidder of one no-trump does hold a four-card major, his reply will be in that major suit.

Take a look at the next page to see how this bidding sequence would look diagrammed. South is the dealer and bidder of one no-trump; North is his partner.

SOUTH	WEST	NORTH	EAST
1 No-Trump	Pass	2 Clubs	Pass
2 Hearts			

By bidding two clubs, North is using the Stayman, and South's rebid of two hearts is telling his partner that he has a four-card major in hearts. Suppose that South has two four-card majors. He would then bid the spades first, and later bid his heart suit.

When the responder has used Stayman to find out if the opening bidder has a four-card major and he is met with a rebid of two diamonds—denying any four-card holding in hearts or spades—he should *not* bid his own four-card major. In order to bid a major, he should have a five-card holding in that suit. If he holds only two four-card majors, he should return to no-trump. If he has 8-9 points, his bid is two no-trump; if he has ten points or more, he should bid three no-trump.

If the responder has bid three no-trump, that will be the final contract for game. If the response had been two no-trump, showing 8-9 points, the opener in no-trump must gauge the situation. This is an easy task—he counts his points. If he has sixteen, that's not quite enough for game, so he leaves the contract at two no-trump. If he has eighteen points, he knows he can go to three no-trump. If he has seventeen points, he looks over his hand. What is the fit? He knows his partner has strength in at least one major suit; so, if he has the other suits well protected, he can venture a three no-trump bid.

Here's another example of Stayman. You are the opener, and you've originally bid one no-trump. Your partner bid two clubs, and you hold the following hand:

♠ 10 6 4 3   ♥ A Q J 8   ♦ A Q   ♣ K 10 4

Here's the bidding so far:

SOUTH	WEST	NORTH	EAST
1 No-Trump	Pass	2 Clubs	Pass

What do you bid? Since you're holding both majors, the normal procedure is to bid spades first. Your spade suit, however, is not a biddable one, and your correct bid is therefore two hearts. If you bid a major in Stayman, it should be headed by at least a queen (though you can stretch that a bit and bid a major headed by a jack).

Other Responses To Opening No-Trump Bids
To an Opening One No-Trump Bid
Here are three other good responses to this opener:

• Pass. The one no-trump opening bid is not forcing, and if you find yourself with a complete bust, it's perfectly fine to pass. What do I mean by "a complete bust"? Here's an example:

♠ 9 7 4 3 2   ♥ 8 6 4 3   ♦ J 9 4   ♣ 10

With this hand, you'd pass and hope that the one no-trump bid does not get doubled for penalty. You don't want to go any further with this junk. One no-trump is high enough with this holding as the opener's partner.

• Respond with two of a suit other than clubs. This response shows an unbalanced hand— a five-card suit—and no interest in going to game.

• Bid four of a major suit. This response requires 7-9 points and a long major suit (by long, I mean at least six in length). This is a shutout bid, and the hand will be played in either four hearts or spades.

To a Two No-Trump Opening Bid

Remember, an opener at two no-trump must have 22-24 high card points. Therefore, if you, as the responder, have as little as four points, the total of both hands is at least twenty-six—sufficient for game. Below is a guide for responses to two no-trump opening bids.

With balanced distribution:

- **4 points:** Pass.
- **4-8 points:** Raise to three no-trump.

Even if you have the maximum of eight points, you know there's no possibility of slam. Your partner's twenty-four points and your eight points add up to thirty-two points, still one short of the slam requirement, which is thirty-three points.

- **9 points:** Raise to four no-trump. If your partner has the maximum of twenty-four points, your side may be able to go to slam.

- **10 points:** Your side is looking at slam, unless your partner has the absolute minimum of twenty-two points. You should first bid a suit; then raise to four no-trump. This is stronger than just bidding four no-trump (as you would do with nine points); it lets your partner know that you have ten points.

- **11-12 points:** Bid six no-trump. Going strictly by the point count, you'll have at least thirty-three points, even if your partner has the minimum holding of twenty-two high card points. If he holds as many as twenty-four points, you still don't have the total of thirty-seven points necessary to bid a grand slam (seven no-trump).

- **13-14 points:** First bid a suit; then bid six no-trump. This is stronger than a direct bid to six no-trump. If your partner has the maximum holding of twenty-four points, he should bid seven no-trump. If he has only twenty-two points, he'll pass your six no-trump bid.

- **15 points:** In your hand, you can go directly to seven no-trump. Even if your partner has a minimum holding of twenty-two points, together you hold thirty-seven points. This means that your opponents don't hold an ace.

With unbalanced distribution (anything less than 5-3-3-2 distribution, such as 6-1-2-4):

• If you have a solid six-card major suit, bid it, no matter how few points you have in your hand. For example, if you held a strong heart suit, your response would be three hearts.

• If you have at least four points in high cards and a five-card major, bid that suit at the next level.

• If you have eight points in high cards and a six-card major, jump raise to four in that suit.

To a Three No-Trump Opening Bid

When your partner opens with three no-trump, you know that she is holding between 25-27 points in high cards. Your first thought is a slam, either small or grand. Count the high points in your hand, and see whether your combined total can be as high as thirty-three for the small slam or thirty-seven for the grand slam.

Follow these guidelines:

• **7 points**: Bid four no-trump.

• **8-9 points**: Go directly to a bid of six no-trump. Your side will have thirty-six high card points at the maximum, not enough for a grand slam.

• **10-11 points**: First bid a suit and then rebid six no-trump on the next round. Some experts use the convention of bidding four diamonds in this spot strictly as an artificial bid. This bid is stronger than a direct bid of six no-trump which fully states your hand. If you go directly to six no-trump, your partner takes it as a shutout bid and will not bid higher. But first bidding four diamonds alerts him to your 10-11 points. If he has twenty-seven high-card points, he can then go to seven no-trump.

• **12 points**: Bid seven no-trump. Even if your partner has the minimum of twenty-five high card points, there's no ace out against your side.

Responses to Opening Bids of Two in a Suit

The opening bid of two in a suit is forcing to game. No matter what the responder holds, he cannot pass. Here are some common responses open to the responder in such a situation:

• *Two no-trump.* This is a very weak bid, showing a poor hand. It is both a negative and artificial bid; it tells the opener, "I have nothing or next to nothing." But this doesn't let the responder off the hook. The opener will usually make a rebid showing a second suit, rebid the original suit, or raise the no-trump response. The original responder is now forced to make another bid. He cannot just let the bidding die out.

Let's follow a sequence of bids to see what happens after a weak two no-trump response. As South, you are the original bidder of two spades. Your partner, North, re-sponded with two no-trump. You hold:

$$\spadesuit A K Q J 6 5 \quad \heartsuit A K Q 9 2 \quad \diamondsuit 3 \quad \clubsuit 4$$

Your correct bid now is three hearts. You intend to end up in game in either major, and now you wait to see which major your partner prefers (you'll know from his next bid). If he bids three spades, your final contract will be four spades, bid by you. If he bids hearts, your contract will be in hearts.

Suppose he now responds with three no-trump, showing no interest in either major suit. What should you do? You end the bidding with four spades. It's your strongest major and you are at game contract.

• *Three of the same suit.* For this response, you need 7-8 points, along with adequate trump support. Unlike the response of two no-trump, which is negative, this is a positive response, inviting your partner to explore slam possibilities.

• *Three in another suit.* This is a natural bid showing strength in that suit. If you name a major of five or more cards in length, you should bid it twice, to show its strength. If the original opener (your partner) has a fit in that major, he will bid to slam, with that suit as trump. Again, you need 7-8 points to bid a new suit in this fashion. This is a positive response.

• *Three no-trump.* This response shows at least nine points and no suit to bid. In other words, the responder has no biddable five-card suit, and he doesn't hold at least four cards in the opener's suit. The following is a hand with which you should respond in three no-trump after an opener's bid of two hearts:

♠ Q 7 5 4   ♥ 8 6   ♦ K 9 8 7   ♣ A 9 5

There are nine points in high cards here, no biddable five-card suit, and your heart holding is weak. This doesn't end the bidding, how-ever, since now the opener knows that with his twenty-five point holding and his partner's nine points, he has enough to try for slam.

7. REBIDS

Opener's Rebids

An opener's rebid can be defined as the second bid of the opener. In this section, we're dealing with suit bids that began at the one level, such as one diamond or one spade. The rebid is an important part of the bidding process; it often determines just where the contract is going—to a partial score, to game, or to slam.

After the opener's partner has responded, the opener has a choice of rebids. We'll examine the responses one at a time and determine just what rebid the opener should make in each situation.

After a One Over One Response

To remind you, a one over one response indicates that the responder has six to seventeen points and four or more cards in the bid suit. As the opener, here's what you do:

- With **13-15 points** and a balanced hand, rebid one no-trump.
- With a strong five-card suit and **12-16 points**, rebid the opening suit.
- If you hold four cards in the responder's suit and **12-16 points**, rebid her suit.

Let's look at a good example of that situation. You hold these cards:

♠ Q J 9 5   ♥ A Q J 6 4   ♦ A 7   ♣ J 4

You've opened the bidding with one heart and your partner has responded with one spade. Your best bet here is to support the responder's spades by bidding two spades.

• With **17-19 points**, jump bid to two no-trump or jump in your own or your partner's suit. For example, if you opened with one diamond, your partner responded with one heart, and you held eighteen points and a four-card heart suit, you'd jump to three hearts.

• If you hold a relatively balanced hand with **19-20 points** and four cards in a responder's major suit, jump to game in the responder's suit.

The following diagram would show the bidding to game in this situation. You are South and the opener.

SOUTH	WEST	NORTH	EAST
1 Diamond	Pass	1 Spade	Pass
4 Spades			

• Jump-shift rebid. For example, if you opened with one diamond, and your partner responded with one spade, a bid of three clubs is a jump-shift rebid to a new suit. This rebid shows 19-20 points and an unbalanced hand, and it is forcing to game. Here's a typical holding:

$$\spadesuit\ A J 8 3 \quad \heartsuit 7 \quad \diamondsuit A Q J 5 4 \quad \clubsuit A Q 5$$

You can show your spade fit on the next rebid.

After a One No-Trump Response

By responding one no-trump, your partner has shown 6-10 honor points (high-card points) and no biddable suit at the one level. Here's how the opener should rebid his hand:

• With **12-15 points** and balanced distribution, he should pass.
• With **12-15 points** and unbalanced distribution, he can rebid his suit or a new good suit. The same applies if he holds 16-18 points.

• With **18-19 points,** he should raise to two no-trump or jump to three of a suit—either his originally bid suit or a new good one.

• With **20 points** or more, he should raise to three no-trump or bid at the three-level in a new suit.

Let's examine some representative hands. You are the opener and have opened with one spade, sitting as South. Your partner has responded with one no-trump. You hold the following hand:

♠ K Q J 8 5 4 ♥ K J 7 ♦ 5 ♣ A Q 7

Bid three spades. You have sixteen points in high cards plus two points for the singleton diamond. By jumping the bid to three spades, you are giving your partner the option of going to game. If he holds only six or seven points, he should pass, but with 8-10 points, he should bid four spades and go to game.

♠ A K 10 4 3 ♥ A Q 6 ♦ K 5 ♣ A 8 4

Bid three no-trump. Your hand contains twenty points in high cards, and you know your partner has at least six points, so a game bid is in order.

After a Two Over One Response
Your partner has shown a good suit, with five or more cards, at least ten honor points, and possibly eighteen points (with distribution). Here's how to rebid:

• With **12-16 points,** make a minimum rebid at the two level or rebid your partner's suit at the three level. The weakest of the rebids is two of your own suit. You make this bid when you hold only 12-14 points and want to discourage your partner from going too far.

• With **17-19 points,** make a jump bid at the three level or bid a new suit at the three level. This is a powerful and encouraging rebid.

• With **20 points** or more, bid game or make a bid forcing to game, such as a jump bid in a new suit.

Rebid After a Single Raise in Opener's Major Suit

Your partner's response shows he has 7-10 points and three or four trumps. Here's how you should rebid:

• With **12-15 points** in your hand, pass.

• With **16-18 points**, your response depends upon your distribution. If you're balanced, bid two no-trump; if not, bid three of your suit. If you're thinking of game, you can bid a new suit (which is forcing), and your partner must respond with other than a pass.

• With **19 points** or more, jump to game or jump bid a new suit.

Rebid After a Double Raise in a Major Suit

Your partner has 13-16 points and a four-card trump suit, headed by at least a queen. Here's how you can bid:

• With **12-16 points**, you are aiming for game—a slam is very unlikely. Bid three no-trump with balanced distribution or four in your major suit if you're unbalanced. The bidding will stop at game.

• With **17 points** or more, you're thinking of a possible slam. See details on how to bid in the chapter called *Slam Bidding*.

Rebid After a Triple Raise in a Major Suit

Your partner will have only ten points at best. Unless you can see slam possibilities (you have more than twenty points in your hand and at least three aces), you should pass.

Again, see the chapter on *Slam Bidding*.

Responder's Rebids

Having heard two bids from the opener—the opening bid and the rebid—you, as the responder, should have some idea of your partner's strength. You must now assess your hand and see whether you will attempt to get a part score, a game score, or possibly go for a slam.

Unless you've been forced to keep the bidding alive or to go for game, here's a good guide to follow:

• With **6-10 points**, make one response and don't bid again unless your partner forces you to.

• With **11-13 points,** you can make two bids—you have a decent hand that could very well go to game.

• With **13-17 points**, your hand is equal to your partner's— you could have made an opening bid yourself. With this type of strength, you must be certain that your side gets to game.

• With **18 points or more**, you *must* think about slam. The ideal way to show this strength to your partner is to jump-shift. If you have twenty points, you should be sure of a slam bid—your partner's thirteen points plus yours gives you thirty-three, enough for a small slam.

8. SLAM BIDDING

Correct slam bidding is an essential tool for a bridge player. Many bonus points are at stake everytime there's the possibility of a slam bid and made. In rubber bridge, the bonuses run from 500 to 1,500 points, and they therefore can make the difference between a winning or losing session.

In duplicate bridge, where each hand is important—because your partnership is playing against a large number of other partnerships—correct slam bidding is of the same importance. The side that is able to bid and make a slam correctly will get the most points for this accomplishment.

There are two essential elements involved in slam bidding: strength and controls. A small slam requires that you win twelve tricks, and a grand slam requires that you win all of the tricks, so both of these two elements must be present. **Strength** means a high-point count; **control** refers to absolute domination of a suit or suits with either an ace or a void.

Strength

There are forty points in high cards in the deck, and it's usually essential that the partners in a slam contract have at least thirty-three of them. When the partners bid a no-trump contract, it is *mandatory* that they hold those thirty-three high-card points between them, because power cards are important in no-trump games. There are no trumps; therefore potential losing cards cannot be trumped if someone develops a void.

In suit contracts, the same thirty-three high-card points are not always essential for a small slam. If one partner instead has a void or a singleton, for example, that may be sufficient to prevent the defenders from cashing two tricks and setting the contract. Sometimes the best slam contracts in suits develop from unbalanced hands—where one of the partners has a very long suit, a solid second suit, and a void and singleton in the other suits. One partner may instead have two singletons, as in this hand:

$$\spadesuit A K Q J 8 6 4 2 \quad \heartsuit 6 \quad \diamondsuit 5 \quad \clubsuit A K Q$$

Obviously, this is a very powerful hand, almost able to go to slam by itself, if the declarer had the first lead. But by the rules of bridge, the defenders lead first, and two aces are missing. If the defenders hold the aces and correctly lead those suits, a slam contract here will be set at once, and go down one trick. But if the partner of the holder of the above hand has either the heart or diamond ace, this partnership can certainly bid (and probably make) a small slam. The only hindrance would be a disastrous split in trumps of 5-0 in the hands of the defenders (possible only if this player's partner is also void in spades). This would occur just 4% of the time.

If this declarer's partner has just one trump and one ace, the small slam contract is assured. If the partner has both aces and one trump, a grand slam is assured. Even if the partner has no trumps, this declarer must go for the slam if his partner has one or two aces; he is 96% certain of getting a favorable split in trumps.

Key Cards

We might therefore say that in this instance, the **key cards** to the slam are the two missing aces. If the partner has only four points in his entire hand, but it consists of one of the aces, then at least a small slam can be bid. If the partner has both aces—and therefore a total of eight high-card points—a grand slam can be bid. Without either ace in the partner's hand, *there is no slam, period.* Suppose the declarer's partner held the following hand:

♠ 3   ♥ K Q J 5 4   ♦ K Q J   ♣ J 9 7 5

He has a lovely hand with thirteen high cards and fifteen points altogether, but there's no possibility of slam. The aces are missing.

Other key cards that you must take into consideration in slam bidding are the kings, the singletons, and the voids. As we saw with the aces in the previous hand, they may become more important than mere points. Thus, when a partnership holds the necessary key cards, it may need fewer than thirty-three points to bid a small slam, or fewer than thirty-seven points for a grand slam. If one ace is out against you, but you're void in that suit, you negate the power of the opponent's strength.

Long, powerful trump suits are excellent for slam bidding. Once the opponents' trumps are used up, the smaller trump cards are automatic winners. Likewise, a long and strong second suit is quite valuable, because after all the opponents' trumps are gone, the declarer can then cash in that side suit and win tricks.

When you hold a long, powerful trump suit and a long side suit, your hand will be unbalanced, and you'll probably have a void, a singleton, or a combination of the two. As I've noted, voids and singletons are keys to slam bidding.

Controls

Since the opponents (the defenders) play the first card, leading toward dummy, if they hold one ace in a grand slam contract or two aces in a small slam contract, they may be able to win their tricks immediately and defeat the contract. It's therefore essential to have **controls**, cards such as aces—which rule a particular suit—or voids, which allow the declarer to trump the led ace of the opponents. These cards are first-round controls, and they are always necessary in slams. Second-round controls are also valuable in small-slam bids. A second-round control would be the king of a suit or a singleton, keys that I've mentioned before.

When you're bidding a slam, it's extremely important to notice which controls you do have and realize which ones you are missing. In those instances where you hold all the controls, the slam bid is a breeze. But those are extremely rare situations. Basically, you'll be dependent upon the controls that your partner has—his aces and kings. There are two ways to get information on which controls he's holding: the Blackwood Convention and the Gerber Convention.

Blackwood Convention

This convention, invented by Easley Blackwood in 1933, has been accepted by bridge players the world over as a method to discover how many aces and kings the partner holds. It starts with an artificial bid of four no-trump, called "asking for aces." If the bidder also needs to know the number of kings his partner holds, then he continues with an artificial five no-trump bid.

By the time the bidding reaches this level, the partnership has agreed on a trump suit (or no-trump), and either partner can ask for aces using Blackwood. As a general rule, the partner with the strongest hand will bid the four no-trump, since he will be the only one with a clear picture of just how many aces the partnership holds, once his partner responds. The bidder of Blackwood should already feel that he can make eleven tricks, for he is bidding at a rather high level, and the response will be at the five-level.

Once a player has bid four no-trump, his partner will answer according to the chart below, depending upon how many aces he holds in his hand. When players agree on using Blackwood as a bidding convention, the partner cannot pass the four no-trump bid; he is forced to respond according to the convention. Here are the responses to the four no-trump bid:

No aces or four aces	Five clubs
One ace	Five diamonds
Two aces	Five hearts
Three aces	Five spades

It will be extremely rare for the responder to have all four aces, since by the time the partners have reached this level of bidding, the Blackwood bidder should have at least one ace and probably more. It's therefore acceptable for a "five clubs" response to mean either all four aces or no aces. If showing all four aces entailed a bid of five no-trump, it would preclude that bid asking for kings. After receiving this information about the aces his partner holds, the Blackwood bidder can now ask for kings. The bid to do this is five no-trump, again an artificial bid and again forcing. Here's what the various responses mean to the bid of five no-trump:

No kings	Six clubs
One king	Six diamonds
Two kings	Six hearts
Three kings	Six spades
Four kings	Six no-trump

Let's now go back to the hand I illustrated at the beginning of this section.

♠ A K Q J 8 6 4 2　♥ 6　♦ 5　♣ A K Q

The holder of this hand is missing two aces, and his only interest is knowing if his partner holds one or both of them, so he can bid a small slam or go to a grand slam. Using the Blackwood Convention, he now bids four no-trump.

If his partner responds with a bid of five diamonds, he knows that she has one ace, and the final bid will be for a small slam, at six spades. There's no point in asking for kings with this hand; they'll play no role in improving his prospects for a grand slam. The only consideration here are the aces. If his partner responds with five hearts, he will have an automatic bid of seven spades, hoping that his partner isn't void in trump, and if she is, that the split isn't 5-0 against him. That would be the only way he could lose the contract.

When your partner bids four no-trump, he is asking for aces. You should respond according to the formula above, and name your exact ace holding. If you are void in a suit, you *cannot* bid it as if it were an ace. This will lead to great difficulties, and you'll have a partner who's furious at you. If you hold one ace and you're void in a suit, your response is still five diamonds, showing one ace.

A final note: whoever bids four no-trump is the captain of the ship. That player will know, from his partner's response, just how many aces are in both hands, and if he bids five no-trump, he will have the same information about kings. He must make the final bid; *the responder cannot do so*. If the Blackwood bidder stops at six, that's where the contract will be. His partner, no matter what her reasoning, cannot bid higher. She must obey the captain of the ship and follow his judgment in this situation.

Gerber Convention

One problem bridge players have sometimes had with the Blackwood Convention is that it requires the responder to bid at the five-level, which is sometimes too high for the combined strength of the partners' hands. To avoid this issue, a player named John Gerber developed a variation on Blackwood in 1938. He called it the Gerber Convention, and it's still widely used by bridge players today.

The purpose of Gerber is the same as that of Blackwood; the bidder simply bids four clubs, not four no-trump, to signal use of the convention. Here are the appropriate responses:

No aces or four aces	Four diamonds
One ace	Four hearts
Two aces	Four spades
Three aces	Four no-trump

If the bidder then wishes to ask for kings, he can bid five clubs, another artificial and forcing bid. The responder should then bid:

No kings or four kings	Five diamonds
One king	Five hearts
Two kings	Five spades
Three kings	Five no-trump

Cue Bids

In situations where the Blackwood and Gerber conventions aren't used, a cue bid can also be used to go to slam. When a player holds a void in a suit that won't be trump, a number of experts avoid the conventions for fear of bidding too high. Let's look at a typical situation that illustrates this principle. We'll follow the bidding of two partners, North and South. Here are their hands:

NORTH	SOUTH
♠ --	♠ Q J 8 6 5
♥ A K J 9 8 4	♥ 5 3
♦ A 10 9	♦ K Q J 8 4 2
♣ A Q 10 6	♣ --

We first note that North is void in spades and South is void in clubs. During the bidding, each partner will cue the other as to the control he has in the void suit. I'll mark these cues in bold. The bidding goes as follows:

NORTH	SOUTH
Two hearts	Two no-trump
Three hearts	Four diamonds
Four spades	**Five clubs**
Six diamonds	Seven diamonds

The use of cue bids (four spades, five clubs) was necessary here in order for the partners to reach a grand slam. In Blackwood, if

North had bid four no-trump, South's response would have been five clubs, showing no aces. He had no way to show his void, and the final bid would have been six diamonds. Here, by the use of cue bids, the partners reached a grand slam.

The cue bid can also prevent a slam with the information it conveys. In the next example, North cued his ace of clubs, asking his partner if she wished to go to slam. I'll show the cue bid in bold letters.

NORTH	SOUTH
♠ 10 3	♠ K Q 9 5
♥ A Q J 9 4	♥ 10 6 5 3
♦ Q J 5	♦ K 3
♣ A J 7	♣ K Q 6

The bidding went:

NORTH	SOUTH
One heart	Three hearts
Four clubs	Four hearts

North made his cue bid at the first opportunity—showing his stopper in clubs—and thus asked his partner if there was a chance to go to slam. South, without an ace in her hand, stops at game.

A Word on Bridge Conventions

The game of bridge has existed for many decades, and it has gradually become more complicated. There have been a plethora of bidding conventions invented and popularized by various players, partnerships, and teams. Some are very complex; others are so esoteric that a situation to use a particular convention might arise just twice in one year for a team that plays constantly.

What I've endeavored to do in this book is show you the basic standard conventions that have stood the test of time and are universally played. These include, but are not limited to, Stayman,

Blackwood, Gerber, Five-card Majors and so forth. As you become more experienced at bridge, you might want to study other bidding conventions. You'll first need a steady partner, since you'll find it helpful to study these conventions together. It's of no use to memorize a complex convention only to find that your partner has no idea what it's all about.

As you play more often—especially if you play in duplicate tournaments—you'll be asked to put down the conventions you use. It's perfectly all right to put down the conventions I've taught you. They're valuable tools that will make you a better player. While you may have limited your bidding conventions, you will come across partners who play a number of complicated conventions, some of which you might not even have heard about. It is their obligation to explain them to you if you don't know how they work.

When you play with one partner, you may find that your style of game lends itself to a particular convention or two. Examine them and see if they work for both of you. There are books devoted just to bidding conventions; after some experience, you might want to dip into them. In the mean time, study the principles shown in this book; they'll make you a stronger player.

9. DEFENSIVE BIDDING

Up to this point, we've looked at opening bids and responses. I've showed you just which hands to open at various levels and which responses you should make to those opening bids. I've also taught you rebids, the use of some bidding conventions, and opening bids of a unique nature, such as the pre-emptive bid. We've discussed how to get to slam, the requirements for slam bidding, and conventions such as Blackwood, Gerber, and Cue Bidding that will help you bid slam contracts. Next we're going to focus on defensive bidding.

By "defensive bidding," I mean those situations where your opponents have opened the bidding, and you put in a bid or bids to challenge for the contract. Your bid may come at the first level of bidding or later, and it isn't limited to just suit or no-trump bids. Doubles are valid bids as well, both as penalty bids and as "takeouts," which disrupt the opponents' orderly bidding as you show your card strength.

When the other side opens the bidding, it isn't often that you may be able to interject bids. Your opponents will have the card strength and the initiative in bidding; many times all you and your partner will do is pass, pass, and once more pass, as the other side merrily moves on its way to a game or slam contract. There's nothing you can do about those situations.

Often novices with rather weak hands just throw in a bid, thinking they'll disrupt the bidding process of the other side. They get doubled and punished with over a thousand penalty points.

Goals of Defensive Bidding

When you're bidding defensively, you must be selective. You must find your spots and then act. If you hold some strength in high cards, you should bid for the following reasons:

• You think you have a competitive hand, and you're going for a partial score for your side.

• Your competitive bids drive your opponents into a higher contract than they can make.

• Sacrificing a hand that will go down only a few tricks will be better than letting your opponents make game or higher.

• You're bidding a suit to signal your partner to lead that suit.

Against these factors, you must weigh the word "double" and the dire consequences that word and subsequent actions can entail. You don't want to be overwhelmed by penalty points; again, I urge you to be selective. We'll discuss a number of defensive bidding strategies in this section, and I'll show you how to handle them correctly and get the best results.

Overcalls

An **overcall** is a defensive tactic in which the player to the left of the opener makes a bid of a suit or no-trump. For example, the following is an overcall of one spade by West.

SOUTH	WEST	NORTH	EAST
1 Heart	1 Spade		

If West had a strong minor suit, he could have over-called at two clubs or two diamonds. When the bidder to the opener's left bids this way, he is overcalling at the two-level, and the requirements for an overcall are a little more stringent, because another trick has to be won at the higher level. Here are some requirements necessary for an overcall:

• 13-16 points. With even more points, as you'll see in a moment, you should instead double. Some experts feel that fewer points are necessary if one holds a suit of six cards. Since the overcall is a defensive bid against an opener, the overcaller should be prepared to play the hand if doubled. If he is overcalling at the two-level, he should have six cards in his bid suit.

Another factor to consider is vulnerability. If the opposing side is vulnerable, and you are not, you can stretch the opening strength required down to ten points, with a six-card suit. Thus, when the opponents have a partial score, overcalls are sometimes made at weak point levels. They may be reluctant to double the overcall, wanting instead to bid their own suits and make game.

• An overcall should be made with at least a five- and preferably a six-card holding. As I stated above, when you're overcalling at the two-level, a six-card suit is almost mandatory, because if the bid is doubled, the overcaller has to make that extra trick at the two-level.

• Your honor strength in your bid suit should be at least a five-card suit headed by A-K, K-Q, K-J, or Q-J. Avoid an overcall if your bid suit contains cards such as Q 9 5 4 3. Even a Q-J five-card suit might give you trouble, but if it were Q J 10 9 5 3, the 10 and 9 would strengthen it considerably.

• If your side is vulnerable, you must be more careful with overcalls. A double and a consequential set of the bid hand may carry with it too many penalty points to make the overcall worthwhile. Always feel freer to make an overcall when the opponents are vulnerable and you are not.

Overcalls not only obstruct the opponents' bidding, but they also serve as lead signals to your partner. The defenders always lead first, and the opening lead is rather crucial in many cases—it can determine whether the other side's contract can be set.

Once you overcall, you're directing your partner to lead your bid suit; otherwise he'll lead his own best suit. That's why I showed you how important the honors holding is when you're bidding an overcall.

Let's look at an example.

You are West and not vulnerable. South has opened with one diamond. You hold the following cards:

♠ Q 9 5 4 3   ♥ Q J 5   ♦ 7 6   ♣ K Q 3

You should pass. Your five-card suit is led only by a queen; it's much too weak a suit for an overcall. If you do bid two spades, your partner will lead a spade to you, instead of leading his best suit, which might be hearts or clubs, where your honors would better help him establish his own strong suit.

Look at another example.

Again, South has opened with one diamond and you hold the following cards as West. Your side isn't vulnerable.

♠ K Q J 8 7 3   ♥ 10 9 4   ♦ 7 5   ♣ K 10

By overcalling here, you're stretching the minimum re-quirement a bit. You hold only eleven points, but you have a good solid six-card spade suit, and your bid of one spade directs your partner to lead that suit.

To summarize, an overcall is a fine defensive tool, which serves one or more of the following purposes:

• It may stop the opponents from arriving at a game contract.

• It can be used to outbid attempted part scores or possibly game contracts by the opposing side.

• It has nuisance value and deprives the opponents of the chance to exchange bidding information at a low level.

• It directs the correct lead by your partner into your best suit.

Doubles

When I first described all the possible bids in bridge, I mentioned doubles—both penalty and takeout doubles. The **penalty double** is bid to punish the opponents for bidding too high. You make it when you or your partner feel you can set the contract and garner penalty points. The **takeout double** has different implications; you bid it to show a hand containing opening strength with the possibility of arriving at your own contract. Let's first focus on this type of double.

Takeout Doubles

A **takeout double** is made in low-levels of bidding, and it forces your partner to bid his best suit. This bid allows you to avoid naming a suit before your partner has responded. When you bid a takeout double at the one or two level after the opening bid or in response to the opening bid, provided all the parameters as stated below are met, it cannot be construed as a penalty double.

The following are the parameters necessary to show a takeout double.

• It must be made at the bidder's first opportunity to double an opponent's bid suit. Here's a good example of this:

SOUTH	WEST	NORTH	EAST
1 Heart	Double		

- It should be made only at the one- or two-level.
- The doubler's partner cannot have bid yet.

Let's look at another example of a double:

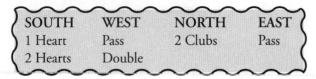

SOUTH	WEST	NORTH	EAST
1 Heart	Pass	2 Clubs	Pass
2 Hearts	Double		

In this example, we see that two of the criteria have been met: the double was bid at the second level and the doubler's partner has not yet bid. But it is not a takeout double. The double wasn't bid at the bidder's (West) first opportunity. It must therefore be interpreted as a penalty double.

Here are the card requirements necessary to make a takeout double:

- At least thirteen points (opening strength).
- Support for whatever suit your partner may bid, if you have no good biddable suit of your own, or a strong suit of your own in which to play the contract.

Let's look at a couple of examples. You are sitting West and South has opened the bidding with one spade. Your cards are:

♠ 8   ♥ K Q 8 5   ♦ K J 9 4   ♣ A J 9 3

You have fourteen points in high cards plus the spade singleton. You really don't know which suit is your partner's best. You'd prefer to play the hand in a major suit (hearts), but you have only four cards in that suit. So you double the one spade bid, forcing your partner to name his best suit. Whatever he names, whether it be clubs, diamonds or hearts (the unbid suits), you'll have sufficient trumps to support him. In this case, if you reach a part or game contract, your partner will play out the hand, since he bid the best suit first. You'll be dummy.

Let's now look at another hand. You're West and South has just opened with one spade. You hold the following cards:

♠ 7 2   ♥ A K J 10 5 4   ♦ A 8 6   ♣ K 3

With two hearts, you may be tempted to overcall, but if you go back to our discussion of overcalls, I set a parameter of 13-16 points to overcall. With more points than that, I stated, a double would be preferable. Here you have seventeen points (fifteen in high cards, plus the two doubletons). The correct bid is a double. No matter what your partner answers, you can always play out the hand in your powerful hearts suit.

Responses to Takeout Doubles

Whenever your partner bids a takeout double, you are required (forced) to respond for at least one round. You cannot pass. In subsequent rounds, you are no longer under any obligation to rebid. There is one exception to this rule, however, and that is a **penalty pass**, with which you are allowing the takeout double to stand as a penalty double.

Let's look at the options open to the takeout doubler's partner.
  • The penalty pass. Pass only if you have a long suit in the opener's bid suit and at least four winning tricks in your hand. Otherwise, you cannot pass.

Here's a situation that would be right for a penalty pass. You are sitting as East, and the bidding was as follows:

SOUTH	WEST	NORTH	EAST
1 Heart	Double	Pass	

You hold the following hand:

♠ 9 5   ♥ K Q J 9 5   ♦ 9 8 5 4   ♣ A 3

With the above hand you can pass. You should be able to make three tricks in hearts and another in clubs. Also, your partner has at least an opening hand and should contribute at least three more tricks. So together you have enough to set the contract of one heart.

• If you have **0-8 points**, bid at the lowest level you can. If the opening bid was one diamond, and your partner doubled, bid either one heart, one spade, or two clubs. If you hold the following hand, for example, a minimum bid would be in order:

♠ 8 5 4   ♥ J 6 4 3   ♦ 6 5   ♣ 8 6 4 2

Basically, your hand is a complete bust, but you cannot pass your partner's double. You must bid something. You bid your best suit and respond with one heart. You're not promising your partner anything, and this bid should tell your partner not to go any further in the bidding, especially if he opened with a minimum holding.

• With **9-11 points**, you can make a jump response. This bid is not forcing on your partner; that is, he need not rebid. If you're faced with the choice of two good suits, choose a major. The next hand illustrates this situation. Again, you are East, and the bidding has gone as follows:

SOUTH	WEST	NORTH	EAST
1 Heart	Double	Pass	?

You hold the following hand:

♠ K J 5 4   ♥ 9 8 7   ♦ 5 4   ♣ K Q 10 9

Bid two spades.

You have a slightly stronger club suit than your holding in spades, but bid the major, even though it's only four cards. Since the bidding was at the one level, your bid is a jump response. It is not forcing on your partner, but instead invites him to try for game in spades if he has a good spade suit and more than the minimum points for opening.

• With **12 or more points**, make a cue bid. **That is, bid the opener's sui**t, showing your partner that your side has enough for game. With less than fourteen points, simply rebid at the minimum level. With fourteen points or more, jump rebid at the next opportunity.

Penalty Doubles

Unlike the takeout double, the penalty double is used to penalize the opposing side for bidding incorrectly. When your partner bids a double, you should be able to judge whether the double is takeout or penalty. Remember that in order to be a takeout double it must be made at the doubler's first opportunity and before you put in a bid. Let's suppose that you are West, and the bidding has gone:

SOUTH	WEST	NORTH	EAST
1 Diamond	Pass	1 Heart	Pass
2 Hearts	Pass	Pass	Double

Even though you haven't yet bid, your partner didn't double at the first opportunity, which was after North's bid of one heart. Therefore you must interpret the double as a penalty double.

A double for penalty is used by good players after an overcall, often with a devastating effect. Even though the double is at an early level in the bidding, it still must be considered as a penalty double, because the doubler's partner has already bid, therefore removing the possibility that the double is a takeout double. The following bidding sequence shows this process:

SOUTH	WEST	NORTH	EAST
1 Diamond	1 Spade	Double	

Since North's partner has already bid, the double is a penalty double. Many novices are afraid to double contracts at the one-level, but doubles of overcalls often yield many penalty points. In this situation, it may be that North has a good hand, with a strong spade suit of his own, and East has a complete busted hand, with just one or two honor points. West may be set several tricks, and, if vulnerable, may be penalized hundreds of points.

When a no-trump contract is doubled, even if the double is made at the first opportunity and before a partner has put in a contractual bid (suit or no-trump) it is considered a penalty double, not a takeout. Remember this: *all doubles of no-trump contracts are for penalty*, even those at the one-level.

Quick Tricks

When they're considering a penalty double, many experts rely more on quick tricks than they do on the point count. A **quick trick** is a trick that can be won on a parti-cular round of play. For example, an ace is a quick trick, since it is the highest ranking card of a suit. An ace and king combined make for two quick tricks, since (unless opponents are void in the suit) their lower ranking cards must fall to these honors. Here's a list of quick tricks:

A K	2 quick tricks
A Q	1 1/2 quick tricks
A	1 quick trick
K Q	1 quick trick
K x	1/2 quick trick

Sometimes these quick values can be increased, depending upon the opponent's bidding. For example, if you hold A Q of a suit bid by the player to your right, who must lead to you, the A Q can be promoted to two quick tricks. The bidder to your right probably holds the king of the suit, and he must play or lead that suit into your A Q. You'll therefore be able to make both the ace and queen as winning tricks.

When that suit is led by any other player, the holder of the king (if he plays it) will lose it to your ace, and then your queen will be the highest ranking card of the suit. If he doesn't play it, then you play your queen and win the trick, since the player to your right can't beat the queen. This is known as a **finesse**—making a trick because of the favorable position of your cards in relation to your opponents' cards.

If the bidder of the suit in which you hold K x is to your right, you can promote the king from 1/2 a quick trick to a full trick for the same reason. Should your partner or any other player play that suit, if the player to your right plays his ace, then your king is now the highest ranking card of the suit. If he **ducks** (doesn't play the ace), then you can play the king and win the trick.

On the other hand, if you hold A Q of a suit, and the bidder of that suit is to your left, you must reduce the quick trick value from 1 1/2 to 1, since a lead through you—that is a lead by the player to your right—will force you to play the ace to win the trick. If you play the queen, it will fall to the bidder's king. Since he bid the suit, you have to assume he holds the king of that suit.

So, using the table above, figure out the number of tricks you can make, adding or subtracting based on the placement of other honors according to opponents' bidding. You must also figure out the number of tricks you can depend on from your partner. You can do this by listening to his opening bids. Here is a quick guide:

One in a suit	He should win three tricks.
One no-trump	He should win four tricks.
Takeout double	He should win three tricks.
Overcall one-level	He should win one trick.
Overcall two-level	He should win two tricks.

If you've opened the bidding, here's another good guide for judging your partner's hand according to his positive responses (bids of suit or no-trump):

One positive response	He should win one trick.
Two positive responses	He should win two tricks.
Three positive responses	He should win three tricks.

Let's now look at a representative situation. You are sitting North, and the bidding has gone as follows:

SOUTH	WEST	NORTH	EAST
1 Spade	2 Hearts	?	

You hold the following cards:

♠ 8 6 ♥ Q J 10 8 6 ♦ A Q 6 2 ♣ K 4

Now, according to the guide above, add up your quick tricks. You get 1-1/2 tricks for your A Q of diamonds, and 1/2 trick for your king of clubs. That's a total of three tricks. Even though the guiding table didn't allow for the Q J of a suit, you hold Q J 10 8 6 of hearts, which will ensure you of three tricks in hearts. Once the ace and king of hearts are played, your Q J 10 will be winning tricks.

In this situation, with your strong heart suit, you are assured of three tricks in trumps. This now gives you five quick tricks. Since your partner has opened the bidding at the one-level in a suit, you can count on her for another three tricks. That gives you eight tricks.

Your opponent's bid of two hearts obligates him to make eight tricks, but by your count, he can make only five. You have a good penalty double here.

Other Requirements

When the bidding by your opponents is at a low level of two in a suit, experts have also figured another way to decide whether or not to double for penalty. You should have the following:

- Ten or more points.
- The ability to win at least one trump trick.
- Shortness in the opener's suit.
- At least 1-1/2 tricks in the unbid suits.

Let's now return to our representative holding to see if it qualifies under these criteria.

♠ 8 6   ♥ Q J 10 8 6   ♦ A Q 6 2   ♣ K 4

The hand holds twelve honor points, at least three winning trump tricks, and 1 -/2 (and possibly more) tricks in the unbid suits. It certainly fits the criteria for a double.

Although correct doubles yield large profits in penalty points, there is a danger in bidding penalty doubles when you feel that you can set the contract by only one trick, after adding up your points and quick tricks. It just isn't worth it to set a contract one trick. Be aware, also, that if you double a major suit contract at the two- or three-level, and your opponents make the contract, you've doubled them into game, which is worth at least 500 points.

At the two-level, it's therefore easier to double a minor suit contract, because it will yield only a part score if made. Count your quick tricks carefully, especially your trump tricks. If you can't make a single trump trick, don't double the contract. If you can make one, and possibly two trump tricks, you are on much surer ground for the penalty double.

Doubling Three No-Trump Contracts

When a player not on lead—that is, not the one who will play the first card towards dummy's hand—doubles a three no-trump contract, he is informing his partner of the correct opening lead.

• If the doubler has bid a suit, his partner must lead that suit, even if he only holds a singleton and has a strong suit of his own.

• If the player to lead the first card has bid a suit, then the double informs him to lead that suit. This happens when the doubler hasn't bid a suit.

• If neither the leader nor the doubler has bid, the lead should be in dummy's first bid suit, unless the leader has a good suit of his own to lead. Let's look at a few examples:

WEST	NORTH	EAST	SOUTH
1 Club	1 Heart	1 No Trump	Pass
3 No Trump	Double	Pass	Pass
Pass			

North wants his partner to lead a heart, and she must open with doubler's (North's) bid suit. One more example:

WEST	NORTH	EAST	SOUTH
1 Club	1 Diamond	1 Heart	Pass
1 No Trump	Pass	3 No Trump	Double
Pass	Pass	Pass	

North has the first lead, and he should play a diamond. Since South hasn't bid a suit, his double requests North to lead his bid suit, which is diamonds.

Doubles of Slam Contracts

When the opponents have reached a slam contract, they can probably make at least eleven tricks, and together they should have strong hands and a good fit. It really doesn't pay to double a slam contract just for some measly points above the line if you can only possibly (without any degree of certainty) set them by one trick. Experts have therefore used the double of a slam contract as a signal to the leader (the one to lead the first card) to make an unusual lead to dummy. By unusual lead, I mean a situation like the following:

Suppose you and your partner have each bid a suit. Depending upon what you're holding, if you're on the lead, you'd ordinarily play a card from your bid suit or your partner's bid suit. But his double is telling you, "Partner, wait a second, lead something else, something unusual."

A typical doubling of a slam calls for the leader to play a card of the first suit bid by dummy, unless that suit is trump. The leader must then lead the suit which was the first sidesuit (not a trump) bid by dummy. For example, suppose we have a situation in which North will be the dummy. The contract is in six spades. South opened with one spade, and North's response was three spades. Then, after South bid four clubs, North responded with four diamonds. After East doubles the final six spades contract, the leader, West, should lead a diamond.

Basically, in most doubles of slam contracts, the signal given is for the purpose of **ruffing**. Ruffing means the trumping of a suit in which a player is void. Thus, in the previous example, East probably was void in diamonds and could cash an ace in another suit to set the six spades contract immediately.

If the doubler is void in a suit, you might ask, why doesn't he just wait to trump that suit when it is played later? The reason is simple. A declarer who knows what he's about, and who sees that there's going to be unbalanced distribution of suits, will immediately draw trumps when he gets the lead, and he will thus deplete East's trumps.

Without trumps, East will be unable to win the diamond trick.

The Immediate Cue Bid

Of all the defensive bids available to you, this is the strongest. It is the equivalent of a two-bid, and it's forcing to game. It promises your partner either an ace or a void in the bid suit.

To refresh your memory, a cue bid is defined as bidding the opener's bid suit. Previously, in the takeout double section, you saw it used as a response to a doubler's takeout bid. Now we're examining it as an immediate bid, instead of in response to a takeout double or overcall. For example, suppose the bidding has gone as follows:

SOUTH	WEST	NORTH	EAST
1 Diamond	2 Diamonds		

The two diamond bid is to be interpreted as a cue bid, telling East that West has a powerful hand. This bid forces East to bid to game. His response will be the same as if West bid a takeout double, so review that section for correct responses. The following would be a typical hand with which to call for a cue bid:

♠ A J 10 4   ♥ A K Q 5   ♦ -   ♣ K Q J 9 8

10. DECLARER'S PLAY

There are several tactical strategies available to the declarer as he attempts to make his contract. The cards he holds, the dummy's cards, the first lead, and the previous bidding by both his partnership and the other side are some of the factors he must review to formulate his correct playing strategy.

Declarer's Strategy

After the bidding is completed, the first play has been made toward dummy, and the dummy has been exposed, the declarer should take time to plan his strategy for playing the hand.

First he should review the bidding in his mind and weigh the information it has revealed. If only one defender bid, the declarer must assume that player has the high-card strength that is missing from both his and the dummy's hands. This isn't always the rule, but it's true often enough to be a logical assumption.

Perhaps one of the defenders opened the bidding. If he opened with a major suit and played five-card majors as a bidding convention, the declarer can assume that he holds five cards in that suit and that his point count in high cards and distributional strength is at least thirteen. With all of this information, the declarer can plan an appropriate strategy.

If one defender doubled the contract and there were no other bids entered by the defenders, the declarer would then have to surmise the reason for the double. Perhaps the doubler has the cards to stop the contract, or perhaps he believes that his partner is holding those cards. A penalty double is a red flag shown to the declarer, and he must adjust his play accordingly.

If neither defender bid, then there is nothing to be learned from the defenders' bidding other than the fact that both players opposing the contract may not have biddable hands or a high enough point count. If the declarer is playing a low-level contract, such as two or three in a suit, it may be that the honors are evenly distributed between the two defenders, so that they weren't able to make a bid. Even passes by the other side convey information to the declarer.

After the opening lead, the declarer should consider the card led before playing one of dummy's cards. Why that lead? Why that suit? Is it a lead from the player's best suit, or is it a lead that hopes to find high cards in that suit in his partner's hand? Is it really the correct lead based on the situation and dummy's strength, or is it the lead of a weak player? This brings us to another point.

One of the factors that the declarer should consider is the relative strength of the players he is up against. Are they good players? Are they experts? Or are they mediocre or weak players? In rubber bridge, after a while, the strength of your opponents will become apparent. In duplicate bridge, where a steady stream of new partnerships come by to play against your side, you will not be so sure of their qualifications.

Let's return to the opening lead. Once the lead is made, the declarer must decide in which hand he wants to take the trick, if he can win it. If he does take the trick, what will be his next lead? To answer these questions, the declarer must examine the cards in his hand and in the dummy and decide on a strategy.

The declarer should first count his winning tricks, then determine what course of play to follow if the sure tricks are not enough to fulfill the contract. Most of the time they won't be enough. He must ask himself which suits are likely to produce other tricks. Will he have to finesse—that is, play a card such as a low card to dummy's A Q holding in the hope that the player to his left holds the king and won't be able to play it? If the finesse succeeds, the queen will hold up as an extra won trick.

The declarer could also try for a ruff—play a suit from dummy that he is void in and trump it. Should he first draw trumps in case the other side is void in a suit, to prevent them from ruffing? If he attacks trumps, will the split be right for him? If there are five trumps out and he holds the A K, will the trumps break perfectly at 3-2 with the queen in the hand holding only two trumps, so that he can establish his other trumps as winners? What will he do if the trump split is 4-1? One guide for him will be the table later on in this section showing the percentages of suit splits.

Here are three basic rules to follow in declarer's play.

The Three Basic Rules of Declarer's Strategy

1. *First and foremost, the declarer must stay alert*. He must remember the bids, the leads, and the cards discarded during the tricks played. He must also keep track of the suits and know precisely how many cards in each suit have been played. Without this knowledge, he will severely handicap himself. He cannot afford to play a guessing game and not really know how many of a particular suit remain to be played. That's a sign of a mediocre player.

2. *The declarer must plan his strategy as soon as possible*. He should have some idea of what he will attempt before the first card is led to dummy, but once he sees that card, and once dummy's hand is exposed, he should immediately plan his play. Knowing what to do, he should then follow through. In case of bad breaks in the suits held by defenders, he must plan an alternate strategy (if possible), which will enable him to make the contract.

If he finds he will be set, the declarer must play to limit the tricks he is set by. At no point during the playing of the hand should he play sloppily or let his mind wander. He must always keep track of the cards and suits played and know just how many cards of each suit remain. I cannot emphasize this point enough.

3. *Declarer must be aware of and play percentages.* He cannot disregard the odds in any situation. If West, an opponent, opened the bidding, the declarer cannot count on East to have all the high cards. If a finesse has only a 50% chance of succeeding, while the chances of establishing a long suit are 68% in his favor, he must try to establish that long suit, and not ignore the opportunity.

Having mentioned percentages, it's a good time now to show you the probability of breaks in the suits.

Probability of Breaks in Suits

As I mentioned before, it may become essential to know the probable division of cards in particular suits held by your opponents in order to fulfill your contract. Of course, the division won't always adhere to the odds, but as a guide to the possible breaks of suits, you should look at the table below. If possible, memorize it.

Suppose you are declarer and hold five of a suit. The dummy also holds five of the same suit. There are three cards out against you in that suit.

How will they break?

Looking at the chart on the following page, you can readily see that 78% of the time the opponents' holdings will be split 2-1. (All of the percentages listed are approximate.)

Number of Cards in Suit Against You	Possible Division of Cards	Percentage
Two	1-1	52%
	2-0	48%
Three	2-1	78%
	3-0	22%
Four	3-1	50%
	2-2	40%
	4-0	10%
Five	3-2	67%
	4-1	29%
	5-0	4%
Six	4-2	48%
	3-3	35%
	5-1	15%
	6-0	2%
Seven	4-3	61%
	5-2	31%
	6-1	7%
	7-0	1%

Let's now examine some of the strategies open to the declarer as he plays out his hand.

Ruffing

To remind you, ruffing is defined as trumping a led suit when you are void in that suit. Let's look at a simple illustration of it. You are South, the declarer, and you're playing the contract in spades.

North
♠ 5 4 2
♥ Q 10
♦ A 6 2
♣ 5 2

West
♠ 8 7
♥ 9 5 4
♦ J 8
♣ A K J 10 9 3

East
♠ Q 10 9
♥ A 8 7 6
♦ K 10 9 5
♣ Q 8 7 6 4

South
♠ A K J 6 3
♥ K J 3 2
♦ Q 7 4 3
♣ -

West leads the 3♣, you play the deuce from dummy, and East plays the queen. Being void in clubs, you ruff the trick by trumping with your 3♠. Now you lead the 7♦ from your hand and win the trick with the A♦ in dummy. You then lead the remaining club from dummy and again trump in your hand. Another ruff trick has been won.

The ability to ruff tricks is a great help to the declarer, and that's why singletons and doubletons are valued when you add the total points in a hand. Of course, they apply only to suit contracts. In no-trump contracts, where ruffing is impossible because there is no trump, you count only honor points to determine the strength of your hand.

Crossruffing

Crossruffing is a way to take tricks by ruffing in each of the partnership's hands, thus using the trumps available separately. In other words, the declarer can lead a suit in which the dummy is void, trump it in the dummy, then lead one of dummy's suits in which he is void, and trump it in his own hand. Use of sidesuits to establish ruffing tricks in both hands is a powerful strategy for declarer. Here is an illustration of successful crossruffing.

North
♠ 5 4
♥ J 10 8 6
♦ 3
♣ A Q 9 7 4 2

West
♠ Q J 6
♥ 5 3
♦ K Q 9 7 6 2
♣ 8 3

East
♠ K 10 9 3
♥ 7 4
♦ A 5
♣ K J 10 6 5

South
♠ A 8 7 2
♥ A K Q 9 2
♦ J 10 8 4
♣ -

East was dealer, and the bidding went:

EAST	SOUTH	WEST	NORTH
Pass	1 Heart	Pass	2 Clubs
Pass	2 Hearts	Pass	4 Hearts
Pass	Pass	Pass	

West led the Q♠, which was won by South's ace. Now, looking over the dummy, South saw that his best strategy was to crossruff. To do this, he had to get rid of the 3♦ in dummy's hand, so he led the 10♦, which drove out East's ace.

East, sensing that declarer was interested in ruffing, and seeing the void in dummy's diamond suit, played a small heart to try to deplete the declarer of his hearts as soon as possible. South won the heart trick in his hand, then led a diamond to dummy, ruffing it by playing a trump from dummy's hand.

Declarer then cashed (won the trick with) dummy's A♣. He discarded a diamond, then led a small club, and ruffed it in his hand. Now he could play another diamond and trump it with dummy's 10, then lead another club from dummy and ruff it in his own hand. Crossruffing back and forth between the two hands, he easily made his contract.

Establishing Long Suits

In order to establish a long suit and take in winning tricks with the small cards in that suit, the declarer must be certain that the defenders cannot trump the long suit. As a precaution, therefore, he should play out trump and exhaust the defenders' trump holdings before he tries to run the long suit. Once the defenders are out of trump, they are helpless to stop the declarer from cashing in tricks in the long suit (provided, of course, that they don't have a stopper to win a trick or two of their own in that suit).

The above strategy works for suit contracts. In no-trump contracts, the defenders, who act first since they have the first lead, will try to establish their long suit. It's often a contest to see which side establishes its long suit first. This becomes vitally important, because a declarer doesn't have to worry about trump. Once the other side is depleted of a suit he still has cards in, he can run all his remaining cards for winners.

In no-trump contracts, the declarer must consider three factors. He must win with his honor cards; he must establish a long suit (if he has one), so his small cards in that suit can be winners; and if he's a bit short on tricks, he must try a finesse or two. This third point brings us to another important declarer strategy—the finesse.

The Finesse

A finesse may be defined as a lead or play toward a broken sequence of cards, such as A-Q or K-J, in order to take advantage of the favorable position of your opponent's card so as to make the trick. The following illustration will make this concept simple. You are South and the declarer. North, the dummy, holds the A Q of diamonds. You play a small diamond toward dummy in the hope of finessing the king, which you believe is held by West.

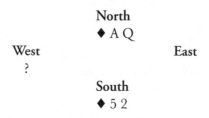

You lead the deuce of diamonds to the A Q. If West holds the king, she's in a bind. If she plays the king, it will fall to the ace, and then your queen will be a winning trick (the highest diamond still unplayed). If West doesn't play the king, you play the queen as a finesse. You win with the queen, and then your ace is boss.

In any event, you will attempt to finesse West for the king. No matter what she plays, you'll play the queen, hoping that East doesn't hold the king. If East has the king, your finesse will fail.

Before you attempt the finesse, you should recall the bidding of the defenders and mentally review their play up to that point. Did West or East enter the bidding? If West put in a bid, then it's more likely she holds the king. Has East avoided leading a diamond when it was his turn to lead? Perhaps he doesn't want to lead away from his king.

You should also ask yourself if there is some other way to win the tricks you need. Should you establish your long suit after drawing out trumps? What kind of split in the remaining cards of your long suit should you expect to find in the defenders' hands? Study the percentage table of possible splits. The more you know, and the more you can reason out the consequences of your play, the better player you'll be.

Entries

An **entry** is a means of securing the lead in a particular hand. In order to enter the hand, that hand must have a card high enough to win a trick, or it must be able to trump a lead to it (by being void in a suit). Here are two simple examples:

1. You want an entry into dummy's hand. Dummy holds the A♣, so you lead a small club from your hand. The ace of clubs is your entry into dummy's hand.

2. Now you want to enter your hand from a lead by dummy. You are void in hearts, and spades are trump. You lead a heart from dummy and trump it in your hand. You've secured an entry into your hand.

There are times when a contract is set because the declarer couldn't secure an entry into one of the hands—either his own or the dummy's—in order to cash the winning tricks that were there. Take a look at the South and North hands in the following example. South is the declarer, and spades are trumps.

North
♠ -
♥ A K 4
♦ 9 6
♣

South
♠ Q J 7
♥ -
♦ J 10
♣

South desperately needs those two heart tricks in dummy's hand, but he has no way to enter dummy if he is leading from his hand. He has no hearts or clubs, and his diamonds are higher than those held by dummy. This situation shows you a good example of a declarer who didn't think through his strategy enough to leave himself with an entry into dummy's hand. He may have played out his minor suits willy-nilly, not realizing that he should have left a higher card in clubs or diamonds in dummy's hand to secure an entry.

A good rule to follow is this: when you're playing a contract, *always make sure that you secure entries into both of your hands—declarer's and dummy's*. If you will need an entry later on in the game, plan for it. Don't use up a valuable entry early on by giving up a high card in a hand that will run out of entries. Entries are valuable; you must carefully preserve them.

11. DEFENDER'S PLAY

When you're defending against the other side trying to make the contract, your first object is to defeat the contract. If the contract can't be set, then your next object is to limit the declarer to just enough tricks to make the contract and not allow him to make overtricks. In rubber bridge, where overtricks are scored above the line, this is somewhat important. In duplicate bridge, where you and all other partnerships in your category (either West-East or North-South) are judged by how well you defend against a particular contract, it is essential.

When you're playing duplicate bridge, the difference between a top score and a mediocre one often boils down to an overtrick. If your partnership is defending against a contract and you allow an overtrick, while all the other partnerships, playing the same cards your side held, limit the other team to just the contract itself, you'll end up with low score. In duplicate bridge, every trick counts. As you become experienced at bridge and have a steady partner, I suggest that you hone your skill at duplicate bridge.

The most important defensive play is the opening lead, since the correct lead often ends up setting the contract, while the wrong lead allows the declarer to make the contract easily and possibly make one or more overtricks as well. So, let's begin our discussion of the defender's play with a study of opening leads.

Opening Leads - Choosing the Suit

As you know, the defenders lead the first trick, and the lead falls to the player to the left of the declarer, who leads toward the dummy. The dummy's cards remain closed till the lead is made. Then the dummy's hand is exposed, and dummy is no longer involved in the play of the hand. It is the declarer versus the two defenders.

The first question the leader must ask himself is this: What suit do I lead? Here is a general guidline for choosing the correct suit.

• If your partner has doubled to indicate his preference for an opening suit, lead that suit.

• If there has been no double directing a particular lead, lead the suit bid by your partner.

• If your partner hasn't bid, lead your own best suit. Be careful not to lose control of the hand too early by giving away your strength at the beginning. If your partner has raised your bid suit, by all means lead it.

• If a suit has not been bid, it's a good idea to lead that suit, since it might be the weak point of your opponents, and your partner may have some high-card strength in that particular suit.

If there is more than one unbid suit, determine from the bidding if the dummy has strength in that suit, and lead through the dummy, if possible, rather than to declarer's strength. It is always best to lead through the dummy—that is, to play a card to dummy's strength—rather than to declarer's power. For example, if dummy is holding A Q 9 of a suit, and you lead that suit, you're putting the question right to the declarer. Which card should he play? Should he try for the finesse immediately, by playing the queen? Should he try for a **deep finesse** (where three cards are missing—here the king, jack and 10) and play the 9?

On the other hand, if you lead to the declarer's strength, and the declarer is holding the A Q 9 of that suit, then you're putting your partner in a bind if he's holding the K 10 of that suit—you're effectively helping the declarer finesse him.

• If you're unsure of what suit to lead, it is best to lead through dummy's strength, since, as shown above, that gives your partner the perfect position (third) to play his strong cards.

• If you gathered from the bidding that declarer has a long, powerful trump suit, avoid leading a trump.

• If you learned from the bidding that the opponents have weak trump, and that the declarer will attempt to make a number of tricks by ruffing or crossruffing, then lead trump to deplete their trumps and prevent this from happening.

• If you hold a singleton, lead it if you suspect that your partner is holding the ace and can immediately win the trick and play back the same suit for you to ruff.

• If you have good trump holdings (four or more) and a l o n g side suit as well, lead the long suit and force the declarer to trump. He then weakens his trumps so that at a later time you can establish that long suit.

• Against no-trump contracts, lead your longest and strongest suit, unless an opponent has bid that suit. If your hand is extremely weak, with no suit that looks inviting to lead, try to figure out which suit your partner has some strength in.

Choosing a Lead Card - Suit Contracts

The following are standard leads in expert play:

• From any sequence of honors, lead the top card.
      1. K Q J or K Q 10 - lead the king.
      2. Q J 10 or Q J 9 - lead the queen
      3. J 10 9 or J 10 8 - lead the jack.

In this instance, the same rule would apply to leads against no-trump contracts.

• With a suit headed by A K, lead the king. If your only holding in the suit is A K, lead the ace.

• With a three-card suit headed by A K x or K Q x, lead the king. If the three-card suit is headed by Q J x, lead the queen. With J 10 x, lead the jack.

• In the following instances, if your partner has bid a suit and you lead his suit, do the following:

1. With a three-card suit headed by one honor, such as K 8 6 or Q 9 4, lead the lowest card. If your three-card suit is headed by an ace, such as A 9 2, lead the ace.
2. With a four-card holding and the top two cards in immediate sequence, such as K Q x x or Q J x x, lead the top card of the holding. When you have the A K x x in a four-card holding, lead the ace.
3. If the four-card holding is headed by only one honor, such as J x x x or K x x x, lead the lowest card in the holding.
4. If you're holding only a doubleton, lead the top card of your suit (e.g. if you have an 8 6, lead the 8).

If your partner hasn't made a bid, lead from the following holdings as directed:

• If you're holding three honors in a four-card sequence, such as Q J 10 6 or K Q 10 4, lead the highest honor.

• If you're holding a four-card suit with an honor at the top, such as Q x x x or K x x x, lead the lowest card in the suit.

• If you hold a three-card suit with an honor as the top card (e.g. K 6 3 or Q 9 2), lead the lowest card of the suit.

• If you hold the A K as doubleton, lead the ace.

• If you hold a doubleton such as 10 9 or 9 8, lead the top card of the two-card sequence.

• If you hold any sequence of three cards with an A Q at the top, such as A Q x, A Q J or A Q 10, do not lead this suit. You are depriving yourself of making both the ace and queen as winning tricks by leading away from this holding.

Leads Against No-Trump Contracts

In no-trump contracts, when you have the lead, experts advise playing the fourth-highest card from your longest and strongest suit. This play works to draw out the opponents' high cards in that suit; you hope that your low and middle cards will eventually be set up so you can win extra tricks.

There are a few exceptions to the above rule. When your partner has made an overcall or bid a suit during the bidding and you hold two or three small cards in that suit, play the top card you hold (unless you hold an honor heading a three-card suit). In that case you'd lead the small card. But if you hold an honor as a doubleton, lead the honor.

When your partner hasn't bid, but dummy bid a suit without a response in that same suit by declarer, you should lead that suit through dummy's strength in the hope of finding your partner with strength in that suit.

If your partner doubled the no-trump contract (especially three no-trump) and neither of you has bid, lead the dummy's first bid suit. This is a conventional lead through dummy's strength.

To sum up and review, the following are conventional leads against no-trump contracts when your partner *has* bid:

- If you hold A x x x or K x x x, lead the fourth best card.
- If you hold K x x, Q x x, or J x x, lead the third best or lowest card.
- If you hold A x, K J, Q J, 9 8, or any other similar doubleton, lead the top card.

The following are conventional leads when your team has *not* bid:

- If dummy has bid, lead dummy's suit.
- If you hold Q J 10 x x or A K Q x x x, lead the top card from that suit.
- If you hold A x x x, K Q J x, K x x x, or Q x x x, lead your fourth best.
- If you hold a doubleton, play the higher card (e.g. with 10 x, play the 10; with J 10, lead the jack).

• If you hold a three-card suit, play the highest card—as long as it's not an honor.

Post-Lead Defensive Plays

After the opening lead has been made, you, as defender, can now study the dummy to see what it reveals. You should pause here, just as you would if you were the declarer, to study your strategic goals. Probably you'll have time to think things over while the declarer is seeing the dummy for the first time and making his own plans. From the bidding and from your partner's lead, you should now have quite a bit of information.

Once you've evaluated the situation and decided which tricks you think you take to defeat the contract (if that's possible), you'll beginto play. Here are some general guidelines to help you know which cards to play as a defender.

Second Hand Low

When a card is led on any trick, the next player to act is the second hand, and, as a general rule, he should play low. This tactic is a standard one, used to prevent the opponents from running or establishing a suit. Let's look at an example of this play.

South is the declarer and has the lead. You sit West and the dummy is North. You hold A 8 3 of a suit. The declarer leads a 6 of this suit, and you look at dummy's hand. It holds the K Q 5 2 of the suit.

If you put down your ace, you will give up control of the suit, since dummy's king and queen will then be the highest ranking cards of that suit. If you play low, however, and put down the 3, dummy must play either the queen or king, and you can still gain control of the suit with your ace. If dummy instead ducks with the 5 or 2, your partner could win the trick with a 9.

Suppose, in the same situation, dummy held the K J 5 2 of the suit. By playing low, you're forcing declarer to make a tough decision. If both the ace and queen are out against him, he might play the king, hoping to force out the ace. You still retain control of the suit with your ace, and now your partner's queen might be a winning trick.

Let's assume that you hold the same cards of the suit, A 8 3, and dummy is holding K 5 3 2. In this instance declarer is holding the queen. If you are second to play, and a 6 is led to you, it still pays to play low. By not playing the ace, you're keeping control of the suit. Of course, there are exceptions to this and every other defensive rule, but if you play low on second hand, nine times out of ten you're making the right decision.

Third Hand High

Playing third hand high is another general rule that will prove correct most of the time. When you are third to play, you must endeavor to play high—either to take the trick or to force out higher cards in the fourth hand—which is your opponent's. In the next diagram, you are East. South is the declarer and North is the dummy. Your partner, West, is on the lead.

NORTH
♣ 8 7 2

WEST   **EAST**
♣ K 10 6 3   ♣ Q 5 4

SOUTH
♣ A J 9

On this particular club trick, West leads the 3, dummy plays the 2, and now you play the queen (playing third hand high). If you had played the 5 or 4, South would have won the trick with his 9, and he would retain control of the suit with his ace. By playing the queen, you will either force out South's ace or win the trick. This is a basic example of the effectiveness of playing third hand high.

Covering an Honor with an Honor

As a general rule, you should cover an honor with an honor. By this I mean that you should play a higher honor over it. By covering, you will either win the trick or force out two of the opponent's honors in one play. Each situation is different in bridge, however, and this guideline is not as applicable as second hand low or third hand high. In fact, it may contradict one of these adages. For example, suppose you are West and hold K J 10. Dummy shows A 5 2. South, the declarer, leads a queen. What do you do, play second low or put an honor on an honor?

```
                    NORTH
                    ♣ A 5 2

        WEST
        ♣ K J 10
```

The correct play is to put an honor on an honor. South's queen is covered by your king. If dummy (North) puts down the ace, your jack and 10 are winning tricks.

Here's another example:

```
                    NORTH (DUMMY)
                    ♣ J 10 4
        WEST                    EAST
        ♣ Q 8 7 2               ♣ K 9 5

                    SOUTH
                    ♣ A 6 3
```

The jack is led from dummy. If East covers with his king, then South would win two tricks in the suit.

East should play low. If he covers with the king, South will win with his ace; then a return of the 3 will allow West to win with his queen. But this would establish dummy's 10 as a winning second trick. The difference of one trick in this situation may very well decide if the contract will be made or set.

More Defensive Plays

When your partner leads a suit at his earliest opportunity, he is usually telling you to return the suit when you're on the lead. This is an important concept in defending against no-trump contracts.

The one hand that will be always be open for your perusal during the course of play is dummy's. I already mentioned how vital it is to lead through dummy's strength. If you see that dummy is holding a suit headed by K J or A Q, the missing honor may be in your partner's hand.

If you play that suit through dummy, it may very well be to your side's advantage.

If the dummy is weak—shows no honors—and holds just something like 8 6 5 3 in a suit, and you are to dummy's left, lead up to the weakness of dummy by playing through declarer's strength. This lead will put your partner in an advantageous position and enable him to take in tricks over declarer's cards.

Signals

Since bridge is a partnership game, signals are of utmost importance. Of course, I'm referring to legitimate signals expressed through the play of the cards (not exposing cards or other forms of cheating). In previous sections on bidding, I've shown how bids can be used as signals for opening leads and how opening leads can be used as signals to your partner to play a particular suit.

One of the best playing signals is the high-low signal.

High-Low Signal

When your partner plays high-low, he is telling you to continue the suit you've led. If he's holding a suit like K 9 6 3, he'd first drop the 9 on your led suit and then the 3. This is a high-low signal to continue with the same suit. Sometimes you won't have the luxury of playing an 9 and then the 3. You might have the following cards in a suit: K 6 5 3. In that case, first play the 6 and then play the 3 the next time that suit is led.

When you play a 6 or higher card on partner's led suit, it should alert him to the possibility of a high-low signal. He must examine his hand and the dummy's hand to determine whether a number of small cards are still out in that suit. For example, suppose you play the 6 on partner's led suit, and he sees that he holds the 5 4 of that suit, while the dummy holds the 3 2. He knows the 6 cannot be the start of a high-low signal, since it must be your lowest card in that suit.

In that case, you'd be discouraging him from continuing in the same suit. If the 3 were missing from both dummy's and his hand, however, and he's paying attention, he may now consider that you hold the missing 3, and that the 6 you played was the first part of a high-low signal. Generally, if you have the luxury of playing a middle card such as a 10, 9 or 8, use it for the signal rather than a lower card which might fool your partner into thinking that you're discouraging the continuation of his led suit.

In defending against suit contracts, any high card played by a partner followed by a low card of the same suit on the next lead asks his partner for a continuation of the same suit. This signal usually shows a high honor card, capable of winning the next lead, or a void in the suit, which would allow a ruff to win the trick.

In no-trump contracts, using the high-low signal can establish a long suit, and small cards in that suit can then win a bunch of tricks. Suppose, in a no-trump contract, your partner opens with the lead of a queen, and dummy shows 5 3 of that suit. You are holding the K 9 6 4. You would signal with the 9, telling your partner to go ahead and continue the suit.

If the queen winds up winning the trick, it is because the declarer held up his ace. Your partner's lead of the queen could have been from a sequence such as Q J 10 x or Q J 8 x. Seeing you play a high card, your partner now continues with the suit. He plays the jack, and this time you play your 2—a definite high-low signal. Declarer will either have to play the ace and lose control of the suit or lose another trick. Now, if the suit is led again by your partner, your side's small cards will end up as winning tricks.

This signal has another purpose in no-trump contracts. It shows your partner the rank of another suit in the dummy's hand that you'd prefer he play. Let's take a closer look at what I mean.

Suppose that your partner leads an ace towards dummy's hand and you follow with a high card of that same suit. This signal asks your partner to play to the highest ranking of dummy's suits. If dummy still has all four suits in his hand, then a spade lead by your partner would be in order. If dummy was depleted of spades, then you'd be asking for a heart lead.

Trump Echo

The high-low signal is also known as an **echo**. When played in a trump suit, it's called a **trump echo** (also known as a **trump signal**). This play indicates that the signaller holds exactly three trumps in his hand, and it's made when the third trump can be used to ruff a trick.

When a trump is led (by any player), the defender using this signal plays a middle card. He follows it with a lower card in the trump suit on the next lead of trumps. For example, if a defender holds the 10 6 4 of trumps, he will first play the 6. On the next trump trick, he will play the 4.

This signal becomes important when a defender has the ability to trump a suit (he is void in that suit). When the signaller's partner gets the lead, he should try to ascertain which suit his partner is void in and lead it. Because he saw the trump echo, he must assume that his partner is void in one of the side suits and will trump the correct lead.

You've now learned the essentials of winning bridge, including the rules and conventions of scoring, bidding, and playing the hands. If you study all the material I've presented, you should quickly become an adept bridge player. I'd like to take a moment now to tell you about some common mistakes in bridge—learn them now so you can avoid making them yourself!

12. IRREGULARITIES IN BRIDGE

The following are the most common irregularities in bridge; not all of the possible infractions of the rules can be listed here. For a more thorough look at these, I advise you to read *Laws of Contract Bridge*, published by the American Contract Bridge League.

Failure to Follow Suit

If a player has failed to follow suit—that is, failed to play the same suit as was led when he still holds a card of that suit—it's called a **revoke**. Any player may call attention to the failure and demand that the revoke be corrected. A revoke is established if the trick is finished and the revoking player plays another card. The offending player may correct his revoke without penalty, but he must do so before the trick is completed (a new lead is played).

If a revoke is established, the penalty is two tricks. If, however, after the revoke occurs, the revoking side does not make any more tricks, then the penalty is just the one revoked trick.

Exposed Cards

Any card dropped on the table face up becomes an exposed card and must be left on the table. If the lead is in the same suit, that card must remain on the table and be played. If another suit is led and the player whose card is exposed is void in that suit, then the exposed card must be played to the lead.

If the lead is to a suit other than the exposed card's suit, the offender must play the correct suit, but he must lead the exposed card if he subsequently gets the lead, or he must play it at the first opportunity.

Lead Out of Turn

If it is one defender's turn to lead, but the other defender leads instead, the declarer may accept the lead, or demand that the correct defender play the same suit or play any other suit but that suit. The incorrect leader then returns the card to his hand.

Declarer Leading Out of Turn

Should the declarer lead from his hand instead of from the dummy when it is the dummy's turn to lead, he may replace the card in his hand, provided no other card was played by the defenders, and then lead a card of the same suit from dummy. He does not have to play the card incorrectly led; he must merely follow suit.

Should the dummy be void in the incorrect suit led form his hand, any card may be led from dummy.

Lead Before the Auction is Completed

If a player makes a lead before the bidding is completed, the offender must leave his card face up on the table until the auction is completed. If the card led is an honor (jack, queen, king, or ace), then the offender's partner is barred from the bidding during the auction.

Should the card led be lower than an honor, it becomes an exposed card and is simply left face up on the table. If the auction is bought by the opposing team, the declarer can accept that card as lead, or ask for the offender's partner to lead that suit. He may also ask for a different lead. If he does this, the offender may replace the exposed card in his hand.

Pass Out of Turn During the Auction

Any player making a pass out of turn must pass when it is his turn to bid on the next round of bidding.

Bid Out of Turn

Any player making a bid out of turn (other than a pass) bars his partner from making any bids until the entire auction is over. The offender, however, is not barred and may continue to bid if he desires.

Insufficient Bid

When a player makes a bid, a response, or an overcall lower than the preceding bid of the opponents, he must make the correct bid of the same suit at a higher level. Should he decide not to and instead bids another suit, his partner is barred from any bids for the entire auction.

Claiming All Tricks

When a declarer, during the play of the cards, claims the balance of the tricks, he must announce the manner in which he intends to play his cards. He then must lay his entire hand face up on the table.

If he claims all tricks and does not announce the manner in which he intends to play out the hand, he must play all his top honor cards and take no finesses, unless the finesse was established on a previous play.

13. DUPLICATE BRIDGE

Introduction

Because rubber bridge is dependent upon the luck of the deal, duplicate bridge was devised to eliminate this element of chance. In duplicate bridge, identical hands are played by all participants, which usually consist of eight or more partnerships.

In order for this to be done, each partnership plays either as a North-South team or as an East-West team, and each participant plays the identical hands held by the previous player sitting, for example, as North, if he is North. Thus the relative skill of the players manifests itself without the luck of the deal.

The device used in duplicate bridge holds four hands of a deal. The standard board is usually of metal. On it is an arrow pointing to the North hand. One of the sections designates the dealer, who is the first to bid. The vulnerability of any particular team is also marked.

One of the advantages of playing duplicate bridge is that a player cannot afford either to bid or play sloppily, since each deal is of the same importance as every other deal. Defending a one-diamond contract therefore has as much validity as defending seven no-trump. It may yield more points to the defenders, since there is more likelihood that the seven-no-trump contract will be a lay-down hand, whereas the one-diamond contract might possibly be a mismatch.

Mechanics of Play

Each partnership is designated as either a North-South or East-West team and is assigned a table and number at the outset of play. There will be a duplicate board at the table, with a deck of cards divided into four parts. The cards are put together, shuffled, and dealt out at random, thirteen cards to each player. Once each player gets his thirteen cards, he plays these cards, and all subsequent players at the same position during the session play the same cards.

In order to retain the same cards, when a trick is played, the card played is not put into the center of the table but is put face up in front of the player, and then turned over after the play. If the trick was won, the longer edges face the partnership. After the play of the entire hand, the cards are picked up by each player and put into the slot marked for the player. The North player puts his cards into the North slot, etc. Then one team (East-West, for example) remains at the table, while the North-South team moves to other tables to play against other East-West teams.

Scoring

In duplicate bridge, there are no rubbers to be made. Each game played is a separate entity. If a contract below game is made, there is a premium of fifty points in addition to the actual points. This is so whether or not the partnership is vulnerable. Making game when vulnerable is an additional bonus of 500 points; when not vulnerable, it is 300 additional points.

To facilitate the scoring, a scoresheet is given to each team. It records the *board number* (each board has one), the *pair number* (each partnership is given one), the *final contract*, *by whom it was played*, and the *final plus or minus score* and *who scored it*. After the scores are all in, the team scoring the highest or best score for one side gets the highest total. For example, if there are eight tables, the highest score will be seven (beating the other seven pairs), and so on. The highest total score of a partnership makes that partnership the winner.

The scoresheet is usually folded and kept with the board; it doesn't travel with the pairs. At the end of the game, it is collected by the director of the tournament, and then the scores of all the pairs are totaled.

Laws and Rules

The laws governing duplicate bridge are put out by the National Laws Commission of the American Contract Bridge League. You should consult them for further information.

American Contract Bridge League
6575 Windchase Blvd • Horn Lake MS 38637-1523
Phine: 662-253-3100, Website: www.acbl.org

A Final Word

For those players who have mastered bridge and wish to test their skill at higher levels, I highly recommend duplicate bridge. It is an exciting, competitive game, and through its competitiveness, the player with an open mind can only learn to play even better. You'll enjoy the game most if you have a steady partner with whom you can learn and practice.

14. GLOSSARY

Above The Line - The place on the scoresheet where premium points, honors, overtricks and undertricks are scored.

Auction - The period during which the bidding takes place.

Below The Line - The place on the scoresheet where trick scores are entered.

Bid - A statement during the auction naming a suit, no trump, or a double or redouble, as well as a pass.

Biddable Suit - A holding that meets the minimum requirement for a bid.

Blackwood Convention - A method of bidding to help a partnership reach a slam contract.

Book - The first six tricks taken by the declarer.

Contract - The final bid, with an obligation to win a certain number of tricks.

Dealer - The player who shuffles and deals the cards.

Declarer - The player who plays out the hand for the partnership that won the bid.

Defenders - The players who play against the declarer.

Doubleton - An original holding of two cards in a suit.

Dummy - The declarer's partner, or the exposed hand of declarer's partner.

Duplicate Board - A device for holding the four separate hands of the players.

Finesse - An attempt to win a trick with a card that is lower than one held by the opponents in the same suit.

Forcing Bid - A bid that forces your partner to keep the auction open.

Game - The fulfillment of the contract sufficient to close out a game.

Gerber Convention - A method of bidding to help a partnership reach a slam contract.

Grand Slam - The bidding and making of all thirteen tricks by the declarer.

Honors - The five highest trumps or the four aces in no-trump.

Jump Bid - A forcing bid of two or three over a bid suit.

Lead - A card played by the winner of the previous round of play.

Long Suit - The holding of more than four cards in a suit; the longest holding in any suit in a hand.

Major Suit - Spades and hearts.

Minor Suit - Clubs and diamonds.

No-Trump - A bid to play out the hand without a trump suit.

Not Vulnerable - A description of a team that hasn't won a game towards rubber.

Opening Bid - The first bid of a suit or no-trump.

Opening Lead - The first card led to the dummy.

Overtrick - A trick won by a declarer in excess of his contract.

Part Score, Partial - A trick score total that is less than game.

Penalty Double - A bid which attempts to penalize the opponents for making an incorrect bid.

Point Count - The total of high-card points and distributional points held by a player.

Preemptive Bid - A high opening bid made to shut out the competition.

Rebid - A second bid made by a player in the same suit or no trump.

Redouble - A bid made by the doubled bidder or his partner, increasing the penalties or the trick values in the event the doubled bid becomes the contract.

Response - A bid made in reply to a bid by your partner.

Responder - The player making a bid in reply to a bid by his or her partner.

Rubber - The winning of two games at rubber bridge by one team.

Set - To defeat the contract.

Signal - A legal method of giving a partner information either by a bid or playing of a card.

Small Slam - The bidding and winning of twelve tricks by the declarer.

Squeeze Play - An end play which forces the opponents to make adverse discards.

Stayman Convention - A bid to ascertain whether your partner holds a four-card major.

Stopper - A card which stops the running of a suit by the opponents.

Suits - Any of the four sets of cards in a pack called spades, hearts, diamonds and clubs.

Takeout Double - A double informing one's partner that the bidder has opening strength, or giving other information about the bidder's hand.

Trick - The taking of cards in a round of play either by high card of the suit or by a trump.

Trump - The suit bid by the winner of the auction.

Void - The holding of no cards of a particular suit.

Vulnerable - The side that has won one game towards a rubber.

X - A symbol representing an irrelevant low card of a suit (e.g. A Q J x).